# A PLACE OF YOUR OWN

# A PLACE OF YOUR OWN

How to choose, plan and equip a home

## Pamela Westland
## and Avril Rodway

Elm Tree Books in association with Hamish Hamilton Limited
for the Prestige Group Limited

First published 1973 by
Elm Tree Books/Hamish Hamilton Limited
90 Great Russell Street London WC1
in collaboration with
The Prestige Group Limited

Copyright © 1973
Elm Tree Books/Hamish Hamilton Limited

SBN 241 02278 9

Illustrations by John Brennan


Printed photolitho in Great Britain by
Ebenezer Baylis & Son Limited
The Trinity Press, Worcester, and London

# CONTENTS

# PHOTOGRAPHIC ACKNOWLEDGEMENTS

*Colour :*

Opposite page 24
*Ready-pasted vinyl wallcovering :* Crown
*Tiles :* Amtico
Between pages 24-25
*Wallpaper :* Sanderson
Between pages 24-25
*Cabinets and perspex fittings :* Prestige
Opposite page 25
*Broom cupboard :* Debutante Range/MAC Builders
    Merchants Ltd.
*Carpet sweeper :* Ewbank
*Wire baskets, Minit mop and attachments :* Prestige
Opposite page 48
*Furniture :* Debutante Range/MAC Builders Merchants
    Ltd.
*Bakeware, pressure cooker, copper-clad saucepans, scales,
chopping board and kitchen tools :* Prestige
*Kitchen paper roll holder, linen tea towel, salt box, pasta jar,
pottery cup and saucer :* Things and Ideas
*Vinyl sheet flooring :* Venezuela/Dunlop
*Vymura washable flocked vinyl wallcovering :* ICI
*Window blind :* Cedar/Sunstor
Opposite page 49
*Ham slicer and carving set :* Skyline
*Hi-dome Colour Clad pressure cooker :* Prestige
Opposite page 64
*French Provincial Style range :* Prestige
Opposite page 65
*Stainless steel tableware :* Old Hall
*Glassware :* Bridge Crystal

*Monochrome :*

Page 27
Tube Investments Ltd.
Page 29
*Double glazing :* Everest
Page 33
*Upholstery :* Four Twenty Furniture Ltd.
*Unit furniture :* G-Plan
Page 38
*Continental quilt filled with Terylene :* Mellalieu and Bailey
Page 40
*Paint :* Crown
Page 46
*Wall can-opener :* Prestige
Page 59
*Tool set :* Skyline
Page 62
*Chest home freezer :* Philips
Page 67
*Alveston stainless steel cutlery :* Old Hall
Page 71
*Wallcovering :* Sanderson
Page 73
The Electricity Council
Page 87
*Fabric :* Sanderson

# INTRODUCTION

A place of your own for the first time . . . buying your own property . . . moving house, an exciting and expensive time. There are so many things to remember and think about—bills to pay; lists to make; organisations and people to telephone and write to; questions to ask; decisions to make; advice you need—that it is difficult to know who to ask. Who, indeed, does know all the answers?

If you are one of the great many families who will be moving into a new house this year (and Ministry of Housing figures show that up to 400,000 new houses are built each year in Great Britain) you will need to know where to get the best advice on borrowing money; on finding a solicitor and a surveyor, and what they can do to help you; what services you can call on and who to contact to get everything ready on time; and what to do if it isn't.

If you are one of the even greater number of families moving into a house that has already been occupied, you will need to know whether any grants are available to help you with converting your house; how much it would cost to replan your kitchen; what you would need to pay now and what you could leave until later.

Here, for the first time, in *A Place of Your Own*, is a complete guide to everything you need to know, from the day relatives and friends first ask what you would like for a wedding or moving-in present. Two check lists on pages 91 and 94 show the basic items of household equipment and furnishings that, chosen wisely, will give you years of pleasure and use.

As every housewife knows, the kitchen is the hub of the household, her own workshop. Every minute she can save there is precious time to spend with her husband and family later on. The right equipment and a kitchen planned with your own needs in mind can save both time and money.

Make the most of every minute is our motto. Housework, that word that used to symbolise being tied to boring routine day after day, can be cut to a minimum without anybody but you yourself being any the wiser. Here again, the right equipment for you and the life you lead is obviously a help; so is knowing what is important to do regularly and what can be left. Follow our plan and you will never use the word 'chore' again.

From cutlery to carpets, from kitchen knives or saucepans to bathroom fittings, we discuss things in terms of cost, value and upkeep. And that leaves you more time to enjoy planning and running your home together. In fact, it is almost a game—making your money buy for you the best equipment, the most attractive ambience and, also important, the leisure in which to appreciate it.

# 1. BUYING THE PLACE

Buying a home is usually as much an emotional as a practical decision, as every couple who has started house hunting will know. As soon as you walk in the door, you will get a feeling of belonging, of home, of welcome. All that remains then is to see if you can afford your dream, and if it is worth the price being asked.

Sensible couples will take a long, hard look at their family budget and their hopes and plans for the future, before deciding.

Because the value of property tends to rise, while the value of money diminishes, most couples starting married life will aim to buy a flat or house at some time in the near future. As it is not normally possible to raise a 100 per cent mortgage, even on a high income, it will mean that a deposit of something between 5 per cent and 20 per cent of the intended house purchase price will be needed.

If you have something near the amount you think you will need for a deposit, the next thing to do is to find out what your borrowing power is. It is a good idea, therefore, to have preliminary discussions with a building society, your local council or other source, to find out how much you can raise on the husband's income, or your joint incomes when applicable. You will have your own priorities about the proportion of your income you are willing to spend on owning your own home. To some people, it is the ultimate goal in life which, once achieved, gives them lasting pleasure and satisfaction. They do not mind if money is short to the point of restricting holidays and outings; perhaps making the running of a car impossible for the first few years. Others might take the attitude that 'you're only young once' and not be prepared to make any financial sacrifices for the sake of buying a roof over their heads.

These considerations should be taken into account when deciding on the area in which to look for a home. Generally speaking, though of course there are exceptions, the nearer the property is to main services, shops, schools and buses the higher the price it commands. Thus it is possible to buy a home for a lower outlay, and with lower charges for general and water rates, if it is a little way out of the town. Don't forget, though that this advantage will be offset by higher fares to work, less convenience for shopping, and fewer amenities.

## Raising the Money

The availability of money which banks, building societies, local authorities and insurance companies have to lend against the purchase of property varies considerably according to the general financial situation. Rates of interest charged on the sum borrowed will vary, too. Because of this fluctuation, it is important that you obtain up-to-date information at periods while you are saving for a property, so that you know exactly what the position is.

When money is scarce, you might have more difficulty in raising a loan on older types of property. Any lending source, however, is always wary of issuing a loan against a flat which was not 'purpose-built', that is a house conversion where it might be difficult to ascertain the liabilities of the various owners regarding the structure and shared amenities.

Since there are so many different ways of raising money, and the relative advantages vary considerably according to personal circumstances, such as age, income and the amount of tax paid on it, prospective house purchasers are advised to go thoroughly into each method.

Those with moderate incomes might find that the option mortgage scheme will benefit them. Under this the Government will pay part of the interest on the loan instead of giving income tax relief. There are certain restrictions about converting this type to an ordinary mortgage later on when your income, and therefore income tax payments, has risen, but it is possible to do so.

If you wanted to buy a home for which the purchase price (or valuation, if it were lower) was less than £7,500, and were planning to take out an option mortgage, a building society might offer a loan of up to 100 per cent of this valuation. Here again, it would depend on the national financial situation at the time.

The term which so often used to be applied to buying your own home, 'having a millstone round your neck for the rest of your life', could not possibly be further from the truth. For one thing, for their own protection as much as for their clients', building societies and other sources will not allow intending purchasers to raise a sum which would be out of proportion with their income. As a general rule, societies are likely to advance something like two-and-a-half to three times the annual gross income of the borrower—a total which will normally include regular overtime and bonus payments. If this seems somewhat harsh, it must be remembered that, from their long experience, building societies are far more likely to know what your repayment capacity is than the average young couple setting up home for the first time!

The period allowed for repayment of a mortgage varies according to the age of the borrower, and may be up to 20, 25 or in some cases 30 years. If the property is leasehold, the term for repayment may be shorter, depending on the unexpired term of the lease.

On the subject of life expectancy, most people borrowing the large sum of money involved in property purchase will want to take out an insurance policy to protect their dependants in the event of their premature death. Special term assurance, which policies of this type are called, cost very little in relation to the sum insured and mean all the difference between possible financial hardship and peace of mind for the bereaved. Tax relief is allowed on these insurance premiums and so further reduces the cost.

Local authorities have the power to advance money to anyone wishing to buy or build a property either for his own occupation or for letting. Since the conditions under which local authorities are allowed to do this, and the categories of persons they can consider, vary from time to time, it is advisable to make enquiries at the local authority in the area where you are intending to buy.

According to the buoyancy of funds, banks are sometimes able to offer loans for house purchase, and it is always wise to ask your bank manager whether this happens to be the case at the time. In any event, even if it is not, bank managers are well placed to give general advice on other sources of borrowing.

Some large companies have schemes whereby they can offer their employees loans. If yours does, you will certainly know about it, and will probably find that the terms are advantageous. Watch out, though, for the clause which explains how your debt is affected should you wish to change your job. It would be disconcerting to discover that you suddenly had to repay the whole amount!

It is just possible that you might be offered a private loan to buy a property, perhaps by the person selling it. In all cases of this kind, where money is offered 'unofficially' by private individuals, you would be most unwise to enter into any kind of agreement until you had discussed the matter fully with your solicitor or bank manager. It is sometimes difficult for those who are not professionally engaged in the financial world—or those who just plain can't add up—to assess the relative merits of different terms; what sounds advantageous and a good offer could in fact conceal a deal where the interest rates were abnormally high.

# Estate Agents

Once you have investigated your likelihood of raising the money, you can decide just what type of property you would like to buy, and in what area. Then, by looking at as many properties as you can, begin to compare like with like and build up a clear picture of what represents value and what does not.

The most usual way to set about buying a property is to go to an agent. The more specific you can be about your requirements, the more he will be able to help you. But you must remember that the agent is, in fact, acting for the vendors; they have engaged him and they will pay his fee. So he is under no obligation to help you find a home. But, of course, it will further both his own interests and his clients' if he can encourage you to buy.

By comparing actual properties with the agents' descriptions, you will soon get to know their jargon. 'Convenient to the shops' might mean it is, as long as you have a car; but it might be anything but convenient if it's uphill when you're walking back loaded with shopping from the supermarket. 'In pleasantly secluded surroundings' will mean that it's further than ever from the shops, and 'Suitable for conversion' can cover a multitude of deficiencies.

If you see a property on an idyllic summer day, with bees buzzing round the honeysuckle, ask the neighbours what the area is like in the winter. Does the stream flood into the gardens? Can the bus to the shops get up the hill in frosty weather? Whatever appears to be relevant. It is worth making enquiries like this because we once viewed one, in black ice in March, which faced a village pond, frozen over and looking dream-like with swans and ducks nestling together to keep warm; a perfect Christmas card picture. The same village pond on any weekend in the summer is surrounded by tourists, complete with deck chairs, spirit stoves, transistor radios, and at least 20 knock on the door of that very house every week to ask if they serve teas there!

When you find a property you want to buy, you should make the estate agent—never the owner, if you were introduced through an agent—an offer for it. And, however timid you might feel, you should as a matter of course make an offer lower than the asking price. This is the accepted practice in the house agency business, and it could, if you were not in competition with many other hopeful purchasers, save you several hundreds of pounds. If, of course, the agent refuses anything lower than the asking price, then you will have to consider whether you feel it is worth that much to you.

An obvious disadvantage to the property—which none the less you are prepared to live with—can make your bargaining power stronger. For instance, the older the property, the more likely you are to meet with a favourable reply to your offer. There are fewer people prepared to take on the responsibility of an old house, which is more likely to have defective woodwork, need new window frames or some kind of major installation, such as a modern kitchen. If you decide to have a surveyor's report—and on an old property you would be advised to do so—you will probably find this ammunition enough. Armed with the gloomy details of just about everything the surveyor can find to criticise, you will almost certainly be able to persuade the agent to 'come down a bit'.

When you make an offer, you must always make it 'subject to survey and contract', which covers a multitude of eventualities. It means, for instance, that if you are unable to raise a mortgage or other form of loan you cannot be held to your offer. The same applies if you have a really unfavourable surveyor's report and find that you cannot afford to have the necessary repairs or reconstruction done—or, indeed, if you just change your mind. You will probably be asked to pay a deposit, perhaps £50, when making the offer, but this, too, will be lodged subject to the exchange of contracts, and will be refunded to you if the sale is not completed.

At times, when there are more prospective buyers than properties on the market, and building societies have money to lend, more house owners tend to offer their property for sale privately, thinking, presumably, that they can manage without the help of an agent. This means that they will effect a worthwhile saving (over £150, for example, on a £6,000 property) some of which they might be prepared to pass on to the purchaser. There is no risk in buying a house direct, because you will instruct a solicitor (*see* page 13) and, if need be, a surveyor (*see* page 12), in the usual way.

To find properties without the help of an agent, look in the local newspapers for your selected area; in the national daily, Sunday and evening papers and in specialised journals which carry a high proportion of such advertisements. Or just wander round the district where you want to live; some owners put up boards of their own outside the house, and one enterprising vendor hung a basket outside, filled with duplicated typesheets giving the relevant details, just as a house agent would!

## Auctions

You might find a house that you like, and then discover that it is to be sold by auction. More owners are tending to this method of sale because the element of competition between the buyers at the sale often pushes the price above what might have been suggested by the agent. If

you should decide to attend an auction, and put in a bid, don't be tempted to go higher than you can afford. It might not matter so much if the lot under the hammer is a Victorian chaise-longue. Perhaps a pound or two either way won't break the bank. But every nod or wave of your sale catalogue for a house could mean another hundred pounds out of your pocket, and this could mean the difference between managing your household budget fairly well, and having to scrimp for years.

Before the sale, the auctioneer will ask if anyone has any questions about the property. At this point, you can raise any matters brought to your attention by your solicitor or surveyor. For, since the sale at an auction is legally binding, you must have your solicitor make his searches and your surveyor his inspection before deciding to bid. If, of course, the property is knocked down to a higher bid than yours, you will have wasted that money. It goes without saying that, in the case of an auction, you must also find out from a building society, or other source whether they would be prepared to lend you the money to the limit you are prepared to bid. Most companies will give you a provisional offer of a mortgage in these circumstances.

The case of buying property in Scotland differs from that in England and Wales, which we have been discussing, in that houses are more often sold 'by private treaty'. This way, the owner places a reserve, or 'upset' price on the property and invites those interested to make offers, in writing, by a specified date. On that date, the offers are examined and the property will usually go to the highest bidder. An offer made this way is binding by law, unless you withdraw it before it is formally accepted, so you should not treat the matter at all lightly. Some properties in England and Wales are offered for sale on these terms, so it is important to remember them.

As soon as your offer is accepted in a 'conventional' sale, tell your solicitor and he can start making the necessary investigations on your behalf. At this stage, too—and not before—you should commission a survey if you want one. There is no point in letting yourself in for a surveyor's fees on a property which is promptly sold to someone else. The only exceptions are, as we have said, if you are putting in a bid at an auction or an offer in a sale by private treaty.

## The Brand New House

If your choice is a newly built house, and especially if it is being speculatively built, or is under construction, there are other steps you will need to take to safeguard your interests.

One of the most frequent complaints is that the builder

rarely keeps to schedule. It so often happens that adverse weather, a shortage of building materials or an industrial dispute can put back the building programme, sometimes by many months. In this time, it is quite likely that a wage increase will have been granted to building workers, resulting in a higher purchase price for you. Make sure how you stand in this case before you sign an agreement to buy, either direct with the builder, or through an estate agent. Sometimes the builder will reserve the right to pass on these extra costs; make sure you realise this.

The individual builder and, to a large extent, the price of the property are both likely to govern the amount of flexibility in design you will be allowed. Some builders work on a take-it-or-leave-it policy and will not alter the layout, even to the extent of lowering the level of wall cupboards if you are particularly short; put in extra fittings or a different non-specified type of flooring. And if they do agree to make modifications, some (but not all) will do so at a price that is uneconomical to the purchaser. In this case, it is better either to try to come to terms with the design as offered—which will usually, if the house is one of a number, be at a 'bulk' price—or find a local jobbing builder or specialist tradesman to do the work once you have moved in.

You read much about the serious defects in new houses, but remember that for every scare story, there are thousands of almost completely satisfied customers whose story does not make headlines. But it is wise to take the precaution, before buying a new house, of talking to other residents in the neighbourhood who have bought a house built by the same firm. If they have been reasonably satisfied, then you probably have not much to fear.

Building societies now will give loans only against properties constructed by a builder who is a registered member of the National House-Builders Registration Council. If yours is, this gives you a fair measure of protection. The builder has to pay this Council a fee for each house he builds (and is, incidentally, entitled to pass on this nominal cost to you). The N.H.B.R.C. sends a representative to inspect the house, looking particularly for major structural defects. It also lays down standards of design and construction and requires builders to put right defects which occur within two years of satisfactory completion. The Council itself takes on an insurance against major defects for a further eight years—giving you ten years' protection in all—and will usually insure you against faulty or incomplete work if the builder goes bankrupt.

If the builder is not registered with the Council, you might decide to engage a surveyor to inspect the house. Do this at the outset, so that he can follow the construction from the earliest stage. It is very difficult to detect faults once the house is just waiting for a coat of paint.

# Surveyors

If you will be needing a mortgage or other form of loan to enable you to buy the property, the building society or other organisations will want to have it inspected to ensure that their money is being lent on a sound investment. You should not confuse this, which is little more than a valuation, with the more detailed report you will receive if you instruct a surveyor to work for you. And in any case, you will not be allowed to see the survey prepared for the building society.

The best way to choose a surveyor is to ask the advice of friends or neighbours in the district. That way you are more likely to be put in touch with someone who will confine his report to the details you need to know, without too many qualifying ifs and maybes.

What *are* the details you need to know? If the property you are considering is of the older type, you want to know if the structure, roof, floors, timbers and essential fittings are sound. If they are not, it is important to know how much expense will be involved in putting them right. Your surveyor will not give you an estimate of the cost of such work; you must ask a builder or, preferably, a number of builders, to give you a quote for this. You will also want to know whether the house is well insulated against heat loss, particularly if you are intending to install some form of central heating, or the existing heating system is one of the factors that appeals to you. And in these days when noise from aircraft, road vehicles and other machines obtrudes so much into our daily lives, you will want to know if the property is insulated against sound, or has double glazing.

Don't leave everything to the surveyor. If you possibly can, visit the house on two or three occasions at different times of the day or week. A property we once viewed on a Sunday afternoon, when all was peace and quiet, turned out to be at the very point of a hill where on weekdays heavy goods vehicles changed down gear to make it to the top.

If your prospective house was built after about 1900, you will want a report on the condition and effectiveness of the damp course. Before that, it was not standard practice to build in this layer of waterproof material, and although some earlier houses have had one fitted more recently, you will want to be sure that those without one are free from such trouble as rising damp.

If the house is in a Smoke Control Area, you will need to know whether the fireplaces have been suitably adapted to burn smokeless fuels. If not, this could be a considerable overhead once you moved in.

Finally, and perhaps most important of all, you will want to know whether, taking the general situation of the property and these foregoing factors into account, the asking price, or the one you have offered, is reasonable. If the surveyor finds faults you had not suspected you can use his report as a 'lever' to reduce the price.

For more specialised reports on such things as the electrical wiring (often seriously at fault, to the point of being unsafe in older properties), gas, drainage, or the central heating systems, you might have to call in another expert, though some surveyors will undertake these assessments.

If the surveyor's report leaves doubt about the condition of the woodwork, you could be well advised to get an estimate from one of the firms specialising in treating for damage by woodworm or beetle. They will usually not charge for a survey, but will give you an estimate to treat the house (most convenient to have it done before you move in, if possible). They will also offer a guarantee against further trouble for a period of twenty years. If the surveyor reports dry or wet rot, then the affected timbers will need to be replaced, for there is no cure.

## Solicitors

Although some people, in order to save costs, manage without a solicitor, those who are relatively new to the business of house purchase are advised to put the matter in the hands of a solicitor from the beginning, and certainly to sign absolutely nothing concerning the purchase without consulting him first.

When you have contacted a solicitor (and if you do not already have one or know of one, you can see a list of those who practise in your area in your local Citizens' Advice Bureau, at the town hall or at the local council offices) you should put him completely in the picture about your intentions once you become the owner of the property. Tell him if you hope to use it, or part of it, as a base for business of any kind, as there may well be some restrictive clause; or if you hope to let part of it. Similarly, if you plan to make certain structural alterations, he should be told as he might find it necessary to tell the building society or other sources of this intention. And if the house is an old one, and considered sufficiently important and historically interesting (this can apply even to the tiniest of cottages) to be listed as a 'Scheduled Property' or an Historic Monument, then there would be restrictions about what alterations could be made. In this case, you might find, for instance, that you would not get permission to replace the window frames; that you might not be allowed to build a new extension, and so on.

It is sometimes possible for the purchaser to use the solicitor appointed by the building society. It is worth enquiring because it could save you part of the fee.

Acting on your behalf, the solicitor will make searches to find out any restrictions applying to the house, such as those already mentioned. He will also find out exactly where the boundaries are (they might be where the existing fence is, or on some other undefined line); who has to look after shared fences, hedges or walls; whether, in the case of an attached property, a chimney is shared with a neighbour, and who has to maintain it; and whether, for instance, the electricity or water supplies come across a neighbour's land. If the council or other authority have any plans for redeveloping the area, or building a new motorway, and these could affect part of the land, or, at the very least, the view from the windows, your solicitor should advise you. The time lapse between your making an offer subject to contract, and the vendor's solicitor submitting a draft contract to your solicitor for consideration, gives ample time for all these matters to be looked into.

If the land on which your intended house stands has already been registered with the Land Registry, the solicitor's job is simplified because details of the piece of land, name of owner, details of any mortgages and restrictive covenants will be recorded and available for his inspection. If not, and ownership has to be proved by examining deeds going back (where applicable) at least fifteen years, his charges to you will be a little higher. (See the scale of charges on page 15 that follows in the section *How Much Does It Cost?*)

At present there is compulsory registration of land only in certain areas, but it is planned that all built-up areas in England and Wales shall be subject to the registration within the next few years. This means that such land would have to be put on the register when it was next sold, the buyer being responsible for paying the charges.

If your solicitor finds that everything about the house is straightforward, and that as far as he can see, you are not likely to come up against any obstacles by buying it, you then proceed to the point of exchanging contracts. In the case of an already occupied house, the timing for the completion of the sale and purchase is best left entirely to the solicitor to determine. For you, as the purchaser, could be the last person, or one in the middle, of a chain of buyers and purchasers of any number of properties, with each one relying on the next not to opt out at the last minute.

## Insurance

From the moment you become the legal owner of the property, that is from the time agreed for 'completion', you are responsible to see that it is covered by insurance. It is vital that you do not wait until you move in; it hardly needs pointing out that the house is as liable to be struck by lightning before you move in as after! If a loan is being advanced by a building society, insurance company or other source of this kind, they will in any case insist on a fully comprehensive insurance cover, as they would think it unlikely that you would have personal resources to repay them their money in the event of their security—the property—being destroyed.

It is false economy to under-insure a property because, in ratio to the value of the house, insurance premiums are still relatively low. On the other hand, there is no point in over-insuring, because the insurance company would not pay more than the market price in the event of loss. (If this were possible, it could give rise to unscrupulous speculating on the part of some opportunists!) However, as the value of your property rises, you will need to reassess whether the existing cover continues to be sufficient. But do be sure to differentiate between the value of the property, and the combined value of the property-plus-land. The sum you need to be insured for is the cost of rebuilding the property, as nearly as possible, at current prices—not what you would have to pay for the land as well.

If you are buying your house on a mortgage, the building society will normally insist that you insure the property with the insurance company of their choice. This, of course, simplifies the administration from their point of view and therefore keeps costs down.

For the insurance cover for the contents of the house you can choose any company that offers the terms you want at a competitive price. Before you take out a policy, it is important to be sure that you understand just what risks are covered, for even an 'all risks' policy does not mean quite what it says.

About two dozen insurance companies have standardised their house and house contents insurance policies, offering the same cover on the same terms. These are called, for the purpose of identification, the tariff companies—the so-called 'tariff' being a voluntary one. The British Assurance Association (see page 99) would give you a list of these and other member companies.

House buildings policies from these companies include cover for damage by aircraft, but not if it is in the course of an act of war. A great deal is heard about policies not including damage caused by Acts of God, but these companies do provide cover for storm, tempest, fire, explosion, lightning and flood (though you have to pay the first £15 of the damage unless you pay to delete the 'excess' clause). Cover is also given for damage by riots, strikes, malicious persons acting in connection with any political organisation, but not by ordinary hooligans—vandalism, in other words. Similarly the policies cover you for damage from impact by road vehicles, cattle or horses, but not if they belong to you or a member of your family. Broken window glass or sanitary fittings are covered, but not other breakages. So if, in a fit of pique, you throw a piece of

early Dresden across the room, you will have to replace it from your housekeeping money!

In a vicious winter, insurance against burst pipes and leaking tanks could mean a great deal to unfortunate householders who have not taken proper precautions in home insulation and lagging. The tariff policies offer this, as well as cover for any damage by, say, oil from central heating systems. Perhaps one of the most important clauses of all is cover for personal liability, for example if a passer-by is injured by a falling tile from the roof of your house; and burglary damage to your home is also covered.

If you take out an insurance policy through a broker, it is up to him to find you the best possible terms for the cover you require.

## Improvement Grants

If you are intending to buy an older type of property and carry out certain conversions, restoration or other improvements, you may find that you are eligible for a grant from the local authority towards the cost of the work. This normally applies to the installation FOR THE FIRST TIME of a fixed bath or shower, wash-hand basin, sink, hot and cold water supply, lavatory, and normally up to a maximum of £200. If a house already has some of these amenities, a grant will be made for installing the others. In special circumstances, which the local authority will advise you about, the grant may be increased to a maximum of £450.

Discretionary grants—so called because the decision whether to make them is entirely at the discretion of the local authority—are available to help purchasers wanting to make more extensive improvements to their homes. The maximum grant allowable in these cases is at present £1,000 or £1,200 where the conversion includes a flat providing separate accommodation. This sum is seen to cover up to one-half of the estimated cost of work approved by the authority.

Most local authorities are willing to give an estimate of the amount they are likely to be able to give towards the cost of any improvements you wish to make, before you commit yourself with the builder, so that you can calculate whether it is within your means. Patience, in a case like this, is a virtue, because no grant is payable on any work begun before the authority formally gave its approval. So do not go along to your local council offices and tell them how beautifully you have converted a spare bedroom into a bathroom and the coal hole into a kitchen. They won't give you a penny towards it! It should be perfectly clear that the council will NOT help with the provision of a second guest bathroom, or a magenta-coloured bathroom suite to replace the cracked and broken one you bought with the house.

# 2. HOW MUCH DOES IT COST?

The economics involved in buying a flat or a house can be calculated in three stages. First, as we have described, you will need to ascertain your borrowing power with a building society, insurance company or other source. This, coupled with the amount you have available for a deposit, will determine the type of property you will be able to afford. Of course, not all of your savings can be used for the deposit, and these deductions form the second stage of your calculations. You have to allow for the professional charges incurred when buying a property —fees to your solicitor, surveyor and so on—which, because they have to be paid in cash, must be subtracted from your available resources. In addition, you must allow for road charges, if applicable, general and water rates on the property, removal fees, installation charges (telephone, TV aerials, for instance) and essential furnishings. And, if your property has a purchase price of £10,000 or over, you must pay Stamp Duty, a Government tax which operates on a sliding scale according to the price paid. The minimum charge, on a property of £10,000, is £105·00. Thirdly you need to budget your outgoings against your likely income—'making ends meet'. We deal with this personal budget later in the chapter.

## House Purchase Charges

The following list (correct at time of writing) gives you an idea of the charges payable at the time of purchase of a house costing £7,000 on which an 80 per cent mortgage advance (*i.e.* £5,600) was made:

| | |
|---|---|
| Surveyor's fee (minimum) if applicable | £42·50 |
| Building Society inspection fee | 15·00 |
| Solicitors' conveyance fee | 51·25 |
| Solicitors' search fees, expenses, etc., say | 5·00 |
| Land Registry fees on transfer of property | 17·40 |
| Land Registry fees on registration of mortgage | 8·70 |
| Building Society solicitors' fees | 22·44 |
| | £162·29 |

This estimate is based on the assumption that the property is already registered with the Land Registry. If it is not, the building society solicitor's fees would be £32·00

instead of £22·44. In this hypothetical case, we have assumed that the same solicitor acted for both the building society and the purchaser, and so a saving was affected. If this were not the case, the purchaser's solicitor would charge a fee of £51·25 for a £7,000 house on registered land, and £82·50 if the land were not registered.

Surveyor's fees are not precisely laid down, since the amount of detail required by purchasers varies considerably as, of course, does the size and type of property. It is advisable, therefore, to negotiate the fee with the surveyor in advance.

As we have seen, you are responsible for the insurance cover on your home as soon as you become the legal owner, so this item too, must be budgeted for from the outset. The current rates charged by the tariff companies, for a £6,000 house with £2,000-worth of insured contents are £16·50 per annum at the time of writing, but they and those of the non-tariff companies change frequently, so please check for yourselves.

## Your Personal Budget

Budgeting is a very personal thing, and probably no two couples would agree on the items they consider top priority for spending money.

Whatever one's individual outlook, however, it seems to us that the happiest marriages, and indeed partnerships of any kind, are those unmarred by financial disagreements. It is important, therefore, that couples decide and agree upon their own list of priorities, so that the unhappy situation does not arise where one spends on a picture to put over the fireplace money that the other had allocated for holiday savings.

| *Items which will have to be budgeted for regularly are as follows. We have left space for you to fill in your own details—in pencil, we suggest, to allow for increases!* | £ | per month or quarter |
|---|---|---|
| 1. Mortgage repayments or rent (probably the largest single outgoing in any family budget) | | |
| 2. General and water rates | | |

3. House, personal and motor car insurance
4. Hire purchase repayments, if any
5. Travel to and from place of work
6. Food, milk and household expenses
7. Subscriptions, such as to a professional association, motoring association or club
8. Heating and other fuels
9. Telephone, if any
10. Road tax on motor-car, if applicable
11. Clothes for the family
12. Fares to shops and school, and school meals for any children
13. Maintenance charges (in the case of a flat or maisonette) and ground rent in the case of leasehold properties

Some of these items will probably be paid weekly, like food and milk, possibly fares to work, fares to the shops and to schools and school meals. Other items, like bills from the electricity and gas boards and the Post Office, are payable quarterly, whereas with rates, road tax, subscriptions and railway tickets it is usually up to the consumer to decide the intervals of payment.

In order to help customers to budget for these longer-term payments, banks operate budget account schemes whereby it is possible to work out what your outgoings will be throughout the year, divide them by twelve and pay the monthly amount into the account. This evens out, for example, the cost of central heating fuel so that the payments do not bunch up out of the earnings in the winter period. Anyone who has tried to budget knows how difficult it is, in the warmth of summer, to be strong-minded enough to save up for the cold of winter!

Whatever method of money allocation you adopt, we feel that it is essential to set aside an amount, however small, for holidays and entertainment. Even if at first this latter sum limits you to the occasional outing to the local public house, or cheap seats in the cinema when there is a good film showing, it will keep at bay that 'millstone' feeling about the responsibilities of house-ownership or, indeed, marriage itself. A further sum should be set aside, too, for unforeseeable emergencies: sudden urgent repairs to the roof, a burst pipe or leaking tank, damage to the motor-car or other vehicle, replacing necessary items of clothing which have worn out more quickly than they were supposed to. . . . All these things can and do crop up

and should not be allowed to become a major headache.

If the property has a garden, this will make its own claims on the family budget, with tools, seeds, plants and fertilisers to be bought each season and, if the property is a new one and the garden needs making from scratch, trees, shrubs, paving stones etc. at the beginning. But, of course, part or all of this expense can be recouped by providing your own fruit and vegetables, cutting down on housekeeping and enjoying the incomparable freshness, not to mention pride, of bringing your own home-grown produce to the table.

Where both husband and wife work, many couples decide to use the wife's earnings to pay for the initial expense of buying the large items in the home, household appliances such as refrigerator, washing machine, home freezer, luxuries such as electric blankets, small items like mirrors for the spare bedrooms and extra sheets all round, furniture for the garden and so on. Alternatively, perhaps, it might be possible to set aside a proportion of the wife's income to save towards a bigger and better house, if you have had to start in a modest way. In any case, it is not a good idea to get used to living on and up to two incomes. For if the wife decides to stop working, perhaps to start a family, the loss of her salary might seem like the sudden imposition of incredible hardship.

Pocket money for both husband and wife should be frankly discussed even before marriage, so that each is clear what his and her responsibilities are, and what is left for 'free spending'. Few women, and particularly those who have been used to their own income, like to have to ask for money for a new lipstick or hairset, and least of all for the cash to buy their husband's birthday present!

One policy decision that will have to be taken is whether or not to buy anything on hire purchase. The stigma about this, which used to be prevalent, has now disappeared, for it is recognised that the 'live now, pay later' scheme can benefit young homemakers as long as it is responsibly undertaken. Perhaps the best plan is to make no decision to buy anything on credit until you have carefully budgeted for all the essential outgoings, the holiday fund, the contingency fund and your pocket money. Then, if it seems possible to set aside the weekly or monthly payments without any hardship, you could decide to take out hire purchase agreements up to an agreed (between you) maximum, or on a couple of items only. Then you could see how things go, and resolve to take out no further agreements until one is settled.

## Mortgage Repayments

In any family, the repayments will be the largest item and it is perhaps useful to see from the following table, at a glance, what this is likely to be in your case. The table gives the monthly repayments in amounts at intervals of £500, from £1,000 to £13,000, at rates of interest varying from 7·25 per cent to 9·0 per cent, for a term of 25 years. For comparison, the rates for 20 years and for 30 years are given for a mortgage advance of £5,500; and for the same advance we list the monthly payments on an option mortgage scheme over 25 years, at rates of interest between 4·75 per cent and 6·5 per cent.

## Rates of Interest

| Amount Adv'd £ | 7·25% £ | 7·5% £ | 7·75% £ | 8·0% £ | 8·25% £ | 8·5% £ | 8·75% £ | 9·0% £ |
|---|---|---|---|---|---|---|---|---|
| 1,000 | 7·32 | 7·48 | 7·65 | 7·81 | 7·98 | 8·15 | 8·32 | 8·49 |
| 1,500 | 10·98 | 11·22 | 11·48 | 11·72 | 11·97 | 12·23 | 12·48 | 12·74 |
| 2,000 | 14·64 | 14·96 | 15·30 | 15·62 | 15·96 | 16·30 | 16·64 | 16·98 |
| 2,500 | 18·30 | 18·70 | 19·13 | 19·53 | 19·95 | 20·38 | 20·80 | 21·23 |
| 3,000 | 21·96 | 22·44 | 22·95 | 23·43 | 23·94 | 24·45 | 24·96 | 25·47 |
| 3,500 | 25·62 | 26·18 | 26·78 | 27·34 | 27·93 | 28·53 | 29·12 | 29·72 |
| 4,000 | 29·28 | 29·92 | 30·60 | 31·24 | 31·92 | 32·60 | 33·28 | 33·96 |
| 4,500 | 32·94 | 33·66 | 34·43 | 35·15 | 35·91 | 36·68 | 37·44 | 38·21 |
| 5,000 | 36·60 | 37·40 | 38·25 | 39·05 | 39·90 | 40·75 | 41·60 | 42·45 |
| 5,500 | 40·26 | 41·14 | 42·08 | 42·96 | 43·89 | 44·83 | 45·76 | 46·70 |
| 6,000 | 43·92 | 44·88 | 45·90 | 46·86 | 47·88 | 48·90 | 49·92 | 50·94 |
| 6,500 | 47·58 | 48·62 | 49·73 | 50·77 | 51·87 | 52·98 | 54·08 | 55·19 |
| 7,000 | 51·24 | 52·36 | 53·55 | 54·67 | 55·86 | 57·05 | 58·24 | 59·43 |
| 7,500 | 54·90 | 56·10 | 57·38 | 58·58 | 59·85 | 61·13 | 62·40 | 63·68 |
| 8,000 | 58·56 | 59·84 | 61·20 | 62·48 | 63·84 | 65·20 | 66·56 | 67·92 |
| 8,500 | 62·22 | 63·58 | 65·03 | 66·39 | 67·83 | 69·28 | 70·72 | 72·17 |
| 9,000 | 65·88 | 67·32 | 68·85 | 70·29 | 71·82 | 73·35 | 74·88 | 76·41 |
| 9,500 | 69·54 | 71·06 | 72·68 | 74·20 | 75·81 | 77·43 | 79·04 | 80·66 |
| 10,000 | 73·20 | 74·80 | 76·50 | 78·10 | 79·80 | 81·50 | 83·20 | 84·90 |
| 10,500 | 76·86 | 78·54 | 80·33 | 82·01 | 83·79 | 85·55 | 87·36 | 89·15 |
| 11,000 | 80·52 | 82·28 | 84·15 | 85·91 | 87·78 | 89·65 | 91·52 | 93·39 |
| 11,500 | 84·18 | 86·02 | 87·98 | 89·82 | 91·77 | 93·72 | 95·68 | 97·62 |
| 12,000 | 87·84 | 89·76 | 91·80 | 93·72 | 95·76 | 97·80 | 99·84 | 101·88 |
| 12,500 | 91·50 | 93·50 | 95·64 | 97·64 | 99·75 | 101·89 | 104·00 | 106·13 |
| 13,000 | 95·16 | 97·24 | 99·45 | 101·53 | 103·74 | 105·95 | 108·16 | 110·37 |

### With repayment over a period of 20 years

| £5,500 | 44·11 | 44·99 | 45·87 | 46·70 | 47·58 | 48·46 | 49·34 | 50·22 |
|---|---|---|---|---|---|---|---|---|

### With repayment over a period of 30 years

| £5,500 | 37·90 | 38·83 | 39·77 | 40·76 | 41·69 | 42·68 | 43·67 | 44·66 |
|---|---|---|---|---|---|---|---|---|

### Monthly repayments on option mortgage over 25 years
### Rates of Interest

| Amount Adv'd £ | 4·75% £ | 5·0% £ | 5·25% £ | 5·5% £ | 5·75% £ | 6·0% £ | 6·25% £ | 6·5% £ |
|---|---|---|---|---|---|---|---|---|
| 5,500 | 31·74 | 32·56 | 33·39 | 34·21 | 35·04 | 35·86 | 36·74 | 37·62 |

# Saving

Many couples find it an advantage to save their money with a building society which, they hope, will eventually grant them a mortgage. Most societies offer regular savings accounts for this purpose. Under such schemes a shareholder agrees to save a regular weekly or monthly amount over a specified period of years. A higher rate of interest—$\frac{1}{4}$ or $\frac{1}{2}$ per cent more than ordinary shares—is usually paid on this type of account. When enough money has been accumulated, and the time arrives to buy the property, the building society will do its best to help with a mortgage. The following table shows the monthly subscriptions needed to accumulate a fixed sum of money under a typical scheme offering $5\frac{1}{2}$ per cent to regular savers.

| | Monthly savings needed | | |
| Target | Over 3 years | Over 4 years | Over 5 years |
| £ | £ | £ | £ |
| --- | --- | --- | --- |
| 100 | 2·56 | 1·87 | 1·45 |
| 200 | 5·13 | 3·73 | 2·91 |
| 300 | 7·69 | 5·60 | 4·36 |
| 400 | 10·25 | 7·47 | 5·82 |
| 500 | 12·81 | 9·38 | 7·27 |

Other ways of investing in a building society include buying shares and making deposits. Although building society shares are usually of a fixed amount, that is £1 or £10 each, most societies will accept sums representing fractions of shares so that in practice any amount over £1 may be invested. These shares are issued over the counter or through the post, not on the Stock Exchange. They are payable at cost, plus interest, at short notice. Societies impose a limit of £10,000 on the investment of any one person, that is £20,000 for a husband and wife. If this restriction bothers you, you will not be concerned about where the down payment on a home is coming from!

Deposits are an alternative way of investing in a building society. By law, deposits cannot be accepted on terms of less than one month's notice for withdrawal, although this can be waived in cases of hardship.

Some societies offer term shares or term deposits under which the investor agrees to leave his money with the society for a specified period of time—for six months, or one, two or three years. In return, he receives $\frac{1}{4}$ per cent more interest than is paid on ordinary shares.

Building societies are now able to participate in the Government-inspired Save-As-You-Earn Scheme under which a person who saves regularly every month for five years becomes entitled to a bonus equivalent to one year's savings, and on this bonus neither he nor the society is liable to any form of taxation. At the moment the bonus is equivalent to a compound rate of interest of about 7 per cent per annum, net of tax. If the savings are left with the society for a further two years, the tax-free bonus is doubled. This is a good way of saving for those able to commit themselves over a long period, although if the contributions are stopped a substantial loss of interest is incurred.

Those with a gambler's instinct might choose to put their savings into Premium Bonds, where of course no interest is payable but, instead, there is the many-millions-to-one chance of winning a large cash prize. This, incidentally, is tax free, should it ever come your way.

Enquire at your local post office for details of the Post Office savings bank scheme, and about National Savings Stamps and Certificates. If you open an account in the savings bank scheme, you will pay no charges, as you do with a bank account, but receive a small amount of interest on deposits. This is not normally looked upon favourably as an economical way to deposit money for long periods, because the rate of interest could mean that your money-plus-interest is barely keeping pace with inflation.

Ask at your bank, too, for details of their current and deposit account schemes. A current account is useful to pay in your monthly pay cheque so that you can draw cheques against it to pay household bills and other expenses (unless you have a Budget Savings Account, which has been described earlier). No interest is paid on money held in a current account, and charges are made for the bank's administration of the account. With a deposit account, which you would use for savings, you do receive interest (the rate varies according to the prevailing Bank Rate) and so it is obviously a better long-term prospect.

# Home Security

When so much time, thought, money and emotion has been spent on getting your home together, you will want to take the precaution of trying to keep intruders out.

It is recommended that you fit all outside doors with a mortice or rim lock, preferably carrying the British Standards Institution mark. Fit strong bolts on the inside of all outside doors, as far away as possible from any glass panels. For windows, do not rely on the casement or sash

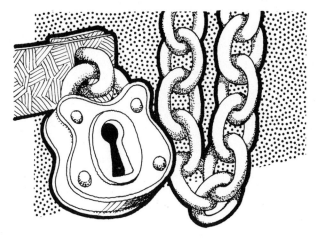

fasteners. On metal windows, have locks fitted professionally; on wooden framed windows, you can probably manage to fit locks yourself.

When you go away, and have to leave your house unprotected, remember to cancel the newspapers and milk in advance and save inviting burglary. Notify the police of your absence and tell the neighbours, too, so that they will not think it is you doing keep-fit exercises on the dining-room floor if they are awakened by unfamiliar noises in the night.

# 3. MOVING IN

It is an exciting, if exhausting, time just before you are moving in to your house. There are a great many things to remember. The timing of decorating, service connection, carpet and furniture deliveries can be critical—and hitches often occur which can throw your carefully worked-out schedules into confusion.

However, if you cultivate a philosophical attitude to the whole affair, make a plan and list the things you would like to have done before moving in, but be prepared for one or two setbacks, you should be able to tackle the job without too much misery and with humour.

## Priorities

If your house or flat has been occupied before, you will have formed a good idea about its decorative state and decided that you can live with the existing colour scheme for the time being, or need to have some decorating done before moving in. If time is short, it is best to concentrate on your main living room, which you will be using all the time, and the kitchen, where it would be more difficult to decorate once large pieces of equipment were in place. The rest could follow once you were living in the house. This is the time, too, to check that existing electric fittings are where you want them, and make arrangements with a local electrician or the Electricity Board to make any changes. If you are moving to a different area, this will, of course, present some problems and you may have to be content to make changes when you arrive.

It is also desirable, before moving in any furniture, to have new floorings and floor coverings in position, either doing the job yourself or commissioning a firm or builder to do it. Allow as much time as possible for this, just in case the manufacturers have sent a box of cork tiles too few, or supplied 27-inch carpet instead of the 9 foot broadloom you ordered!

When you know the date you will be moving in, you will need to get in touch with local Electricity and/or Gas Boards to connect (or re-connect, in the case of old property) supplies for you and install cookers, refrigerators, etc. For the Electricity Board a form must be filled in and they will take a meter reading and check wiring. You will have made sure where your equipment is to go and

that points are available. It is a good idea to draw a rough plan for whoever is installing it so that they will not position anything in the wrong place if you are not there.

If you live at some distance, make arrangements to leave a key with the local estate agent or builders from whom you bought the house and let the Electricity and Gas Boards know where it can be obtained; or you can arrange for them to arrive on the day you move in so that you can supervise them on the spot. If you are buying an electric cooker from an Electricity Board showroom, they will install it free, otherwise there will be a small connection charge. Both Boards are at your disposal for advice and help on any matter connected with gas or electricity supplies.

If the water has been turned off in the house, or not yet turned on in a new house, it will be necessary to get in touch with the local Council to make arrangements with the Water Board. A Water Board inspector will check and pass the fittings, taps, etc. and will arrange for an inspector to turn on the supply ready for when you need it.

## Telephone

Fill in an application for one some time before you move, but don't be disappointed if you have a fairly long wait for installation, unless you can prove that you have special need for a phone. In some areas the telephone service is very overloaded and there maybe a waiting list, or you may be asked to share a 'party line' with another subscriber. This means that two households have access to the same line, and it has its disadvantages. One 'party', by picking up their telephone, can hear the conversation of the other and you may be prevented, at an inconvenient moment, from using your phone by 'Gas-bag, Gas-bag number nine, yacking on the party line'. You do get a small reduction in rental, which does not make up for the inconvenience, but at least it's better than having no telephone at all, and you can always put your name down for a separate line when one is available.

In the first instance, ask at your Post Office for a card to fill in, asking for information or requesting a telephone to be connected. Charges will vary according to circumstances—i.e. how difficult it is to connect wiring, whether there has been a telephone in the house already, the type of telephone (table, wall or trimphone) you choose and whether you require an extension. You can also check, before installation, on the amount of quarterly rental charges and cost of individual calls so you can budget ahead for this if you want to. At the time of writing, installation charge was quoted as anything up to £35, according to the wiring required, with additional charges for an extension phone. Quarterly rental was about to go up to £5·50 for an exclusive telephone, and £4·40 for a shared line.

## Change of Address

Arrange for post to be re-directed to your new address. This involves filling in a form, obtainable from any post office and there is a charge for the service. At the time of writing, the charge is 50p for one month, 75p for three months and £2 for one year, so assess how long it will be before all your correspondents have been informed that you have moved, and make arrangements accordingly. At least a week's notice is required by the Post Office if you want to have mail forwarded.

If you have a car, let the insurers know as your premium might be affected.

If you are going to live in the same area as before, communicate your new address (and name) to your bank, doctor, dentist, newsagent, subscription department of any magazine you take, TV rental firm and so on (see page 23).

However, if you are moving out of the area, arrange to transfer your bank account, subscriptions, etc. in good time. It is really advisable to wait until you are in the new house before registering with a different dentist or doctor as you will want to make some enquiries before doing so.

Lists of doctors and dentists in the area can be consulted at the local post office and it is a good idea to ask

neighbours for their recommendations and suggestions. You can also check on how accessible the surgeries are—depending on whether you have to get there by public transport or can go by car. A long walk to the doctor's surgery in winter when sickening for flu is not a very comfortable experience!

Remember to clear out unwanted belongings and rubbish in your present home some weeks before you move. It's amazing how much one can accumulate even in two rooms! Get rid of anything that could be of use to local jumble sales or Oxfam shop and gradually dispense the rest to the refuse collectors. If there is a heap of things to go at once, it's more considerate to arrange a special collection through the local Borough Surveyor's office.

## Removal

As well as direct deliveries by stores to your new home, you will no doubt have accumulated furniture, wedding presents and personal belongings which must be taken there, too. If the load is large or there is some distance to go, it will obviously be too difficult to move it piecemeal by car and you will have to find a removal firm.

This is a situation where it really does pay to get estimates beforehand as they can vary as much as 90 per cent between different firms. In other words, if the lowest quotation was £30 the highest could be £57! The difference in the 'quality' of the move between a high price and low price firm is not usually very great, so you could really be wasting money by taking the highest estimate.

It would be reasonable to obtain four or five estimates before making up your mind, and check with each firm that they do, in fact, offer a comprehensive service—that is, they will pack and unpack and load and unload your goods as well as actually transporting them.

Your responsibility is to see that the removers take all you want to move and that it is placed in the right rooms in your new house or flat. Read any contract you are offered by a remover very carefully before signing it. If time is short, write to the National Association of Furniture Warehousemen and Removers (*see* page 99) and they can give you names to contact in your area. It might also be worth enquiring if you can move in a 'part load'—that is, sharing van space with other people. It could cost less, but the timing might not be just when you want it, and obviously you would have to go to one of the larger removal firms who would be likely to have the volume of business making such an arrangement possible.

Ask any friends who have recently moved what their experience has been and if they can recommend the firm which did the job for them—this is probably the best way to decide, providing the cost is satisfactory.

Alternatively, you could hire a van and conduct the move yourself, with the help of friends. But it's still just as well to compare prices as it may prove almost, if not fully, as cheap to have it done for you.

How much, if anything, should you tip your removers? Usual figure is about 7½p on each £1 of removal charge and it can be given in a lump sum to divide between the men. There is no obligation to tip, of course, if the job has not been satisfactorily and willingly done.

Don't pay the bill until after the move has been completed and you have checked that everything has been delivered undamaged. It is advisable to insure your furniture for the move, which will not cost you much—around 20p for each £100-worth of cover, well worth it if you are moving antique pieces or expensive brand-new furniture, as generally removers accept little liability for damage done during removal.

To make the job of the removal men easier, label each piece with a different coloured self-adhesive label for each room in the house—blue for living room, yellow for bedroom, etc. and give the men a check list. Then, if you are not on the spot or are busy elsewhere they know where things are to go.

## On the day

Arrange to arrive at your new home equipped with the ingredients for making tea or coffee, or better still a vacuum flask of coffee or tea and one of soup, and with something to eat, even if it's only sandwiches, meat pies and fruit. It's unlikely you will have time for a proper meal until the evening. However well organised you are, there is always plenty to do, or some hitch you could not possibly have foreseen may have occurred. It is not funny to arrive at a new house in the middle of winter and find no electricity or gas connected and no means even of boiling a kettle.

With forethought and luck, however, you should have

your flooring down, main pieces of furniture in the right rooms, equipment connected and services laid on.

Hang up curtains in your main room, bedroom and bathroom for privacy (you have, of course, measured and made them in advance having checked or installed suitable tracks, or improvised some temporary substitute), ask your nearest neighbour to get the milkman to call in the morning for an order—and your new home is inhabited at last.

This check list will help to keep your dates organised. Fill it in in pencil so that you can rub it out and use it for subsequent moves!

| | Date | Firm or Board |
|---|---|---|
| Laying of Carpets | | |
| Laying of Flooring | | |
| Electricity Connection and installation of equipment | | |
| Gas Connection and installation of equipment | | |
| Central Heating | | |
| Water Inspection Turning on | | |
| Decorating | | |
| Forwarding of mail arranged | | |
| Installation of telephone Requested Promised | | |
| Notified of move: Doctor Dentist Bank Newsagent TV Rental Magazine subscriptions | | |

Even on a rainy day, the sun shines in this room. Wherever the outlook is bleak, pamper your illusions by using the colours of spring, summer or autumn with a wall covering such as this daffodil yellow ready-pasted vinyl.

Use of patterned and plain tiles gives a carpet square effect in this simple room. Note how the pattern is cleverly echoed around the walls and on the occasional table. It is a long-lasting and practical idea, needing the minimum of maintenance.

*Not too little pattern, not too much, but just right. . . . A single panel of a dramatic wallpaper frames an old iron bedstead—a possible junk shop bargain—daringly painted in a toning pink. Notice how the use of white for the architraves and accents on the bedside tables, and the neutral carpet, emphasizes the pinks and the purples.*

Two Prestige cabinets (the white one incorporating a safety locking section) and a modern range of simple smoky acrylic fittings enhance these attractive bathrooms.

*This broom cupboard in the Debutante range of kitchen furniture measures 78 by 21 by 21 inches. It comes fitted with shelves and spring clips, holding the Ewbank carpet and floor sweeper, Minit mop and broom handle. Inside the doors, Prestige plastic-covered wire baskets tidily store cleaning materials, and another portable basket is at the ready for the daily jobs around the house. (See page 48 for more details of the cupboard's arrangement.)*

# 4. KEEPING WARM

Given the choice, what form of heating should you choose for your home? Whilst tradition dies hard and the idea of a coal or log fire is appealing, most people these days will want at least to consider some form of central heating. It is convenient and efficient, and it adds value to the house.

What exactly is 'central heating'? Not so long ago, a simple explanation that heat was generated from a central boiler and distributed to the whole house by means of pipes, radiators or warm air ducts and grilles would have sufficed, but of course there are now some other systems of whole-house heating which would not fulfil these terms of reference—such as, for example, night storage heaters. So it is, perhaps, advisable to break the term 'central heating' down into different sections and define each a little more closely.

Full central heating implies that the whole of the house, including areas such as halls and corridors, is heated. It should be automatic, in that it needs attention no more than a couple of times a day (although many systems, of course, using time switches and controls, are completely automatic). It must be able to heat living areas to at least 65 degrees F–70 degrees F and bedrooms to 55 degrees F –60 degrees F when the outside temperature stands at 30 degrees F. The following are considered comfortable temperatures for main rooms:

| | |
|---|---|
| Living room | 70–75 degrees F |
| Bedroom | 60–65 degrees F |
| Bathroom | 65–70 degrees F |
| Hall | 60–65 degrees F |

Background heating provides lower temperatures throughout the house and extra 'spot' heating is usually required in very cold weather. The heating device is not of sufficient power to maintain overall temperatures of more than, say, 55 degrees F or so.

Part central heating, as its name implies, provides heating from a central device to part of the house only.

It is essential, before committing yourself to any particular system, to obtain from the installer an exact definition of what it can do in the context of your house, an estimate of cost for installation and running costs, based on current fuel prices. This might well affect your choice of appliance, taking into account the length of time you intend to stay in your house. For instance, you might find that a system which was quite cheap to install had high running costs, so that over a period of, say, five or six years you had spent more than if you had a more expensive system with lower running costs. The question of resale value of your house would also have to be taken into account—full central heating can add about 90 per cent of its cost to the value of your house when selling. Another point to raise at an early stage is what maintenance will be required. It is often advantageous to pay a fixed sum for regular maintenance and repair, depending on the system.

You will probably find yourself faced with one of the following alternatives to consider when the subject of home heating is under discussion.

1. Newly built house or flat with choice of central heating system to be decided by you.
2. Newly built house or flat with a standard central heating system installed by the builder.
3. Newly built house or flat with heating as an extra cost.
4. Existing small house with no central heating.
5. Existing large house with no central heating.
6. Existing house with adequate central heating but not what you would have chosen either for convenience or running costs.

It is clearly better, if it can be managed financially, to have central heating installed at the building stage. You will be able to pay for it as part of the mortgage, it is cheaper and easier to install and you will avoid a certain amount of mess and upheaval inevitable if it is put in later on.

If points 1 and 3 apply to you, spend as much time as you can to find out about the systems available. Friends will often be able to give valuable information on running costs, effectiveness, convenience and so on, whilst Gas and Electricity Boards, the big oil companies and individual firms can help with costings and the amount of heat your particular house will require.

The National Heating Centre in London (address on p. 99) which exists 'to provide impartial and unbiased advice on all aspects of domestic heating' might well be the organisation to consult if you really can't make up your mind on the best system to choose. The Centre, which receives support from fuel authorities and manufacturers, but not a Government grant, provides a number of services.

There is a permanent display of many different boilers, radiators and other ancillary products. A library containing literature relating to literally thousands of different products provides a good starting point if you wish to investigate the various systems available. Write and ask for literature, but try to be specific in your request.

Consultations are available at the Centre, by appointment, for a reasonable fee. If you are unable to visit the Centre, write and ask for an Analysis Form. This is a very comprehensive questionnaire which, when correctly completed, will enable the Centre to recommend the size and type of system best suited to your particular requirements and circumstances.

A Register of Engineers is maintained by the Centre. All installing engineers who are registered are legally bound to install systems in accordance with written standards and provide a two-year guarantee, backed by insurance—a very necessary cover, especially if the engineer should, for any reason, cease trading before the expiration of the guarantee. Under a scheme called PLAN 4, both the customer and the engineer can have their interests protected. The cost of the installation is paid by the customer to the Centre before the work commences and is held pending completion. When the job is finished, it is checked by an authorised inspector, and providing that the system is satisfactory, payment is released by the Centre to the engineer. If for any reason the installation requires modification or completion, then payment—at least in part—is withheld.

Charges are made for some, but not all, of the services and you are advised to write for details.

If your house comes under 2, you may find it a financial advantage to accept the standard heating offered unless you are very definite about it not being the type you want. Identical heating systems installed in a number of the same type of estate house may come considerably cheaper to each purchaser than if every house had a different system. There will probably be a saving in time, too. Check exactly what is being offered, where grilles or radiators will be placed. You may find that an extra radiator or towel rail could be added if necessary at a small extra cost. If you plan to move in any case in a few years, the odds are it will not be worth making too many costly alterations to existing plans.

You may, however, find that you are considering buying an old house which has no central heating at all. This fact may well be helping to keep the price down at a level you can afford—and shouldn't deter you from buying if the house is otherwise what you want.

**A small old house** presents few problems and can be heated comparatively cheaply even without central heating. A modern oil convector for instance is good looking, economical to run and can give up to the equivalent of 3 kWs of heat. It would be suitable for the average living/dining room and on moving to a larger house, you could use it in a garage/workroom—or during power cuts! Or buy fan-assisted electric heaters which soon warm up a room.

**A large old house** presents more of a problem, especially if some of the doors and windows are not particularly well fitting. This may be a house you are intending to improve gradually, because it is soundly built and will reward any work you put into it. If full central heating throughout is not possible, it might be a good idea to start off with a couple of electric night storage heaters in the main rooms. These heaters can gradually be added to as funds allow and 'spot' heaters such as an infra-red heater in the bathroom or an extra electric or oil convector heater which can be moved round as the need arises, can be used in cold weather. In these circumstances, please read carefully the section on home insulation (*see* p. 28)—you may feel that some of the money you have available might be spent on this to advantage at an early stage.

Perhaps the most irritating heating problem occurs when you have found a delightful house which you want to buy and live in for some time. It is centrally heated and you are paying for this in the purchase price, but the system is not what you would have chosen; you consider it expensive to run or the radiators are in the wrong places for your furniture arrangements. It hardly seems an economic proposition to have it pulled out and replaced, but you wonder if it won't always be an annoyance to you. This is basically something only you can decide, but on the whole it probably pays to cultivate the optimistic attitude that you will be able to afford replacement later on.

Now for a look at the different systems of heating and what they have to offer. Depending on the budget and also on what you consider essential to your comfort, you have many choices open to you.

## Central Heating

There are, obviously, many ways in which the heat you are intending to buy can be distributed from a central source. These fall into three main groups.

1. Hot water circulates through small-bore pipes, forced through by an electric pump, from a central boiler which may be gas, oil, solid-fuel or electric, to radiators or skirting heaters. This type of system is suitable for new houses or can be put into existing ones. The pipes are so small that little construction work is involved.

2. Electrically produced heat, charged at cheap, off-peak

rates, is stored and given off again when required. Distribution of heat can be either from storage heaters or through the floor or ceiling. It can be used either as background or full heating. It is obviously expensive to install underfloor heating in existing houses, but night storage heaters are practicable anywhere and are available in many good designs.

3. Warm air, heated by a central heating boiler or direct air-heating furnace (electric, gas, oil-fired, solid fuel) is circulated through ducts and grilles.

Choice is as individual as buying a new dress or shirt and will depend greatly on your house and finances. Don't go in for cut-price, door-to-door offers of central heating, but consult the fuel boards, major oil suppliers, National Heating Centre, or other reputable authorities who will recommend reliable installers. As with most projected large expenditure, it is worth getting several estimates before you begin. Three should be sufficient.

*Oil*  Generally speaking, an oil-fired system is the most expensive to install, but running costs are very competitive. As it is a financial advantage to buy oil in bulk, you will need to have space for a large tank somewhere in your garden—and the ingenuity to disguise it if necessary!

*Solid fuel*  This can still be the cheapest form of central heating to run, particularly if you have room to store plenty of fuel bought at low summer rates. However, you must be prepared with most boilers for the regular chores of carrying fuel and emptying ashes. There are many very efficient boilers available.

*Gas*  A very popular source of domestic heating as no fuel storage space is needed and special tariffs are available to keep the running costs down. If built into a new house and a 'balanced flue' boiler is used, no chimney flue is needed. There are many different systems available and your local Gas Board can give you advice to fit your particular needs.

*Electricity*  One of the cheapest forms of heating to install in a new house as it involves no pipework, fuel store or chimney, but unless off-peak electricity is used, it can mean comparatively high running costs. The following make use of off-peak electricity:

a. Night storage heaters, mentioned earlier, can be installed one room at a time as the budget permits, and can be either 'controllable' so that you can regulate the heat output, or 'uncontrollable' when heat is emitted when the unit is not actually storing it. These heaters tend to be slightly bulky, but can be placed in a suitable alcove or incorporated into the wall structure of a new house.

b. Central Electricaire units with ducting replacing the pipework, and grilles in each room instead of radiators. This is a comfortable form of heating, but more suited for installation when the house is being built.

c. Underfloor heating, which consists of cables embedded in an insulated flooring material which stores off-peak electricity (in some systems, the cables are withdrawable in case of any future faults). This again must be put in when the house is being built and only directly heats the ground floor.

d. Ceiling or panel heating is also available, but is not so common as the systems previously mentioned.

Central heating is a very competitive business and, if you are not including costs in your mortgage, you should be able to make arrangements to pay for the installation on deferred terms. Enquire what facilities are available at the outset as many companies offer special facilities. Some oil companies will estimate for you the likely cost of fuel for a year, and allow you to pay for it monthly or quarterly to spread the cost, the balance, if any, being adjusted each year.

*Time switches, etc.*  If you are going in for a mechanical system of heating, it seems logical to plan also for a time switch which can be set to any timing you want, and in

*Thermostatically controlled fan convector radiators can be linked to hot water central heating systems and can be used instead of conventional radiators. The model shown here has a natural teak effect surround*

fact many systems incorporate these as a matter of course. After setting, your heating is switched on and off automatically at the most convenient times for you. This and the question of placing of thermostats (to help decide the general temperature level of the house) should be discussed at an early stage with the heating engineer who is doing the job for you. Also, you will undoubtedly need hot water for kitchen and bathroom in summer, although the radiators are cold, and all this must be allowed for at the time of installation. Some systems do not, in fact, provide for this separation of heating and water systems.

It is often an advantage to have humidifiers to keep the air moist if you have a central heating system, and these can range from simple appliances which you keep topped up with water and hang on your radiators to more complex pieces of electric equipment. If you have precious antique furniture they are very necessary indeed, and in any case many people complain of dry air with central heating and humidifiers can remedy this.

Incidentally, it is worth having alternative means of heating (and cooking) however minimal they are, in case of power cuts. A small convector and supply of paraffin (use in greenhouse or garage to get value for money) and a camping cooker which will be useful for picnics can give a wonderful sense of security.

*Less costly heating*    If you can't run to full central heating at first, investigate the possibilities of one of the following:

*Solid fuel plus*    If you have a house with an old-fashioned and inefficient open fire, consider replacing it with an efficient stove or fire with a back boiler and two or three radiators. This will supply heat for your main room, heat upstairs and domestic hot water.

*Oil-filled electric radiators*    These look very like hot-water radiators but are oil-filled and heated by electricity. They can be bought one at a time, are thermostatically controlled and are cheap to install, only needing wiring for electricity if necessary. They can, however, be rather expensive to run.

*Electric skirting heaters*    These can replace existing skirtings or be screwed to them. Vents allow the passage of air over a heating element; it then rises to warm the room. The heaters are bought by the foot and are suitable for any room in the house.

## Insulation

Whatever form of heating you eventually choose, you can help to make your house more comfortable and cheaper to keep warm if you insulate it effectively against the cold.

In other words, the right place for the warmth you are paying for is in your house, not escaping through the roof, walls or windows.

This can be done in a variety of ways—by double glazing the windows, by cavity wall and loft insulation, by the use of insulating ceiling tiles, wall linings and so on. Even if the expense of double glazing seems out of the question at first, you may feel it well worth while finding out about it and other forms of insulation for future reference.

*Loft and wall insulation*    An unglamorous and unseen way of spending money on the house is to lay it out on loft and cavity wall insulation, but the benefits can certainly be felt in increased comfort and lower fuel bills. Always consider the whole question of home insulation BEFORE putting in central heating, as it can save on the cost of the system you choose by cutting down on the number of radiators or size of boiler you will require.

It is not too difficult to insulate the loft yourselves and there are several products on the market which the amateur handyman (and woman) can use. One type consists of insulating granules of vermiculite or loose mineral wool which are poured between the joists in the loft. Another is a roll of special fibreglass or mineral wool insulating material, available in different thicknesses, which is unrolled to fill the same space. The thicker the 'wool', the higher the degree of insulation. In an old house, with irregular distances between the joists, the loose filling might prove more economical.

If your loft is close-boarded on the floor, perhaps to use as a store or extra room, you can still insulate by using special insulating boards nailed to the rafters, or aluminium foil tacked to them.

When working in a loft you will need a short length of board to kneel on between the joists, as you must avoid stepping in the spaces between them. If you don't, you might find your leg protruding through the ceiling of the room below! Take a strong torch or cycle lamp with you and wear old clothes. It is advisable to wear gloves when using some insulating materials as they can cause discomfort or a rash on the hands.

Make sure your insulation is deep enough—two inches is the recommended depth for fibreglass and three inches for rock wool, mineral wool or vermiculite chippings.

It's a good idea to ask your local builders' merchant's advice on the quantities of material you will need, see if he will sell to you on a sale or return basis—and overorder slightly. It is maddening to find that you have just too little material to complete the job.

When you are insulating the loft, it is also necessary to lag the top and sides of the cold water tank and water pipes at the same time. Clearly, if no heat is coming up from the house below, there is a much greater risk that they will freeze during the cold weather. You can use tank-lagging sets for standard size tanks, or a fibreglass blanket. There are various tie-on or clip-on laggings for pipes, or wrap lengths of insulating material round them.

Another form of insulation is cavity wall insulation, that is, filling the space in the centre of the walls with a special insulating material of foam plastic. Holes are drilled through the outer wall and the material is pumped in in liquid form. It quickly sets to provide an excellent insulation. This job, however, must be done by a qualified team and several firms offer a service. One firm claims that between 20 per cent and 30 per cent of 'paid for' house heat can be lost through non-insulated cavity walls, and that the money saved in fuel would soon cover the cost of having the insulation professionally done.

There are several other jobs you can do yourselves which will help to keep the house cosy. You can put up thin expanded polystyrene sheets (available from wall-paper shops) on the walls and these can effectively be papered over (make sure, however, that you buy the non-inflammable variety). These sheets, the manufacturers claim, keep rooms snug by eliminating the cooling effects of circulating air touching cold walls, and cut down on condensation. Polystyrene ceiling tiles are also effective and worth using in kitchen and bathroom.

Draught-proofing doors and windows is another do-it-yourself comfort-maker. Start with the front and back doors and any French windows first, using either a metal strip (long-lasting and effective but not the easiest thing to put on) or plastic foam strip (short-term but easy to apply), or a rubber or plastic piping strip. Treat windows in a similar way, and fill up any cracks between frames and brickwork with a sealing material such as putty or plastic wood. Draught excluders for the bottoms of doors are also effective.

Finally, if you are making curtains, look out for a special lining which has a coating of fine aluminium particles that reflect heat, thus cutting down on heat loss from the room on winter nights. It costs little more than an ordinary good-quality curtain lining and is available from most stores. It should be made as a detachable lining, as it needs dry cleaning rather than washing.

*Double glazing*  Most people talk rather vaguely about 'double glazing' meaning simply a sandwich of two layers of glass in the window-opening instead of one piece. However, there are basically three types of double-glazed window.

  *a.* 'Insulating glass', which consists of factory-made units. These are basically either two pieces of glass held together with a metal alloy or plastic spacer, or

*Double glazing keeps the heat in and the cold air out. Here sliding secondary windows eliminate draughts and help to maintain an even temperature in the nursery*

two glasses edge-fused together. Both look like a single sheet of glass and are hermetically sealed so that you will still only have two surfaces to clean.

  *b.* 'Coupled sashes' consist of a single window with an auxiliary window fitted to it. These can be separated for cleaning purposes, and it is often possible to fit blinds between the two panes.

  *c.* 'Secondary windows' are simply added windows. They are usually tailor-made for existing houses, and are available in different variations. They can be fixed, hinged or sliding, with ventilation facilities of various sorts. These secondary frames can usually be lifted out so that they can be stored during the summer.

You will find that some manufacturers provide a fixing service, and in fact this is essential with many forms of window. Those who don't will supply very detailed fixing instructions.

There are also several methods of do-it-yourself double glazing available using special channels, either metal or plastic, to hold the second pane of glass. These are then fixed to the window frame with special plastic clips and screws. Most large stores and some chain stores supply the channelling.

There are several advantages of fitting double glazing, apart from the saving in fuel costs.

1. As the 'cold window area' is virtually eliminated, the whole room space is evenly warm and usable.
2. There is usually less condensation in a double-glazed room than in a single-glazed one (of particular advantage in kitchen or bathroom).
3. If there is a wide enough space between the two panes of glass, there will be a certain reduction of noise from outside.

Most people who have lived in double-glazed houses emphasise the increase in comfort above everything else, although they admit that they enjoyed the other advantages too.

It is a good idea to start double glazing gradually with one or two rooms and have other rooms done as you can afford it. As most people's requirements are very individual, only a general picture of double glazing can be given, but the Insulation Glazing Association exists to give more detailed advice and the names of member firms in your area. You will find its address on p. 99 and also the addresses of other firms who specialise in insulation services.

# 5. FLOOR COVERINGS

You're lucky indeed if you can start your married life with a house furnished from top to bottom, just as you would like to see it. For most people, it is a question of spending money on priorities, and a mistake at an early stage may prove to be costly. Generally speaking, if you have to work to a budget it is better to concentrate on making your living/dining room really attractive and inviting, ensuring that you have a comfortable bed, and buying the best you can afford in basic kitchen equipment, cutlery and china.

However, it is a good idea to plan your furnishings complete from the beginning, even if you can't buy them all at once. You will be surprised by the generosity of friends and relations when the wedding presents start coming in— and of course they will want to give you things which will fit in with your furnishing plan.

Remember that a few well-chosen pieces of furniture, interesting ways of decorating and clever improvisations can add up to a more attractive whole than matching suites and wall-to-wall carpets throughout in badly-planned settings. Intelligence and forward-planning ARE needed. However much you like a particular pattern of china or cutlery, for instance, it's no use buying it unless you are sure you will be able to get replacements in three years' time when your husband has broken a couple of cups and a plate or you have managed to throw away one of the best knives with the vegetable parings! If the retailer can't reassure you that the pattern will be available for a long time to come, it is worth the trouble of writing direct to the manufacturer yourself.

Perhaps the only comfortable chairs you can afford are not the ones you will eventually want in your drawing room—but choose something which can, perhaps with a little refurbishing, be used elsewhere later on. A second-hand sofa, for instance, with a new cover could be your first solution to comfortable seating. Later it would make a great addition to a nursery—for children's play as well as mother's comfort. A pretty cane chair could eventually move into a garden room or spare room.

Light fittings are often expensive to buy and go out of fashion fairly quickly, yet they are important focal points in your room. An antique lamp is a good investment if you can find one reasonably priced, as it will fit into any setting, modern or antique, will not date (it has already!) and

possesses an elegant presence which can draw the eye from other shortcomings in your décor.

Here are some more detailed hints to help you in deciding on such important items as flooring, beds and bedding, lighting, china and cutlery, and so on for your home.

## Choosing Floor Coverings

Flooring is one of the most expensive items you will have to consider and it needs considerable thought to make sure you are buying the right thing. Whilst it is (comparatively) easy to change wallpaper or paint colours if you don't like them, your carpet or flooring, once down, is there to stay for a long time. Plan it first, bearing in mind that a loud pattern or assertive colour will be more difficult to furnish around and live with than something more subdued which relies for its attractiveness on its weave or texture. You will, of course, want your floorings to be warm, easy to clean, nice to look at, quiet and non-slip—or at least to possess some of these qualities, depending on which room you are considering.

Before you even start thinking of carpet, tiles or whatever, look at your basic floors. First and foremost they must be dry and flat, and if you are moving into an old house with damp, bumpy floors, get expert advice from a local builder on putting them right. Wood floors must be stable and have no nails sticking up. If you laid a carpet on rickety floorboards, you would be asking for uneven wear and would considerably shorten its life. If it is really too difficult to even up your floorboards, it would be well worth covering the floor with hardboard before laying carpet or tiles.

Any kind of carpet needs a good underlay to give it resilience and help it to wear longer, and beneath the underlay should come a layer of clean dry newspapers to prevent dust being sucked through cracks in the floorboards when vacuum cleaning. Some carpets do, in fact, have their own 'built-in' underlay, or you can buy separate felt or foam ones. It's particularly important to have underlay stair-pads to help cushion the wear on this heavily-trafficked part of the house. Thin PVC or lino flooring will also need a special paper underlay if put down on board floors, or the cracks between the boards will show through.

*Carpets* For comfort, ease of cleaning and good appearance, most people would undoubtedly choose to have a fitted carpet in their living room; but in an area subject to such continuous and heavy wear it must be a good quality one. The temptation to buy cheap carpeting which looks good at first but will not wear well is very great if the budget is limited. It would, in this case, be much more satisfactory to buy a good carpet square and stain or polish the surrounding boards or lay a linoleum surround. The carpet square could be moved from time to time to even up the wear.

But how can you tell a good-quality carpet—apart from the price? It is particularly difficult now that so many synthetic fibres are used instead of, or mixed with, the traditional carpet material, wool. Wool has many good qualities. It has a natural springiness, is easy to clean, does not soil readily and is difficult to set on fire. In modern carpet manufacture it is now often used mixed with a synthetic or man-made fibre such as nylon to give it even harder-wearing qualities, a usual mixture being 80 per cent wool and 20 per cent nylon. Acrylic fibres such as Acrilan and Courtelle come close to the qualities of wool in appearance and behaviour and are available in many attractive colours and designs. Rayons, too, are often mixed with wool to add bulk, but as they have not the hard wearing qualities of either, carpets made entirely of rayon are best avoided in areas of hard wear such as stairs or living rooms, although they would be quite suitable for bedrooms.

Tough sisal carpets can now be bought in a wide range of lovely subtle colours, are relatively inexpensive and will wear for years—although they have not the softness of a pile carpet.

You will also find, when you are looking round the stores, that there are other categories of carpet such as the needlefelted kind which are not woven but have a flat surface, or carpet tiles made from animal hair which are very easy to lay, soft and extremely hard-wearing. The latter have the great advantage that you can replace the odd worn tile when necessary as they need not be stuck down, and if they are laid with the pile going alternate ways they give a pleasant shaded effect. A rush mat would be a good buy for a kitchen or bathroom as it does not like very dry conditions and responds well to having water dropped on it; these mats come in attractive patterns and are inexpensive.

You will find that you can buy carpet in many widths. Popular broadloom widths are 15 feet, 12 feet and 9 feet. Strip carpets are in standard widths of 36 inches and 27 inches and stair carpet widths are 18 inches, 27 inches and 36 inches, the 27 inches width being the most generally popular. With luck, you may find that one of the range of broadloom widths will fit your room measurement.

It will be useful to know the metric equivalents which are the standard conversions agreed by the carpet industry and are 'rounded off' to give a convenient figure.

$$27 \text{ ins.} = 69 \text{ cm.} \qquad 9 \text{ ft.} = 275 \text{ cm.}$$
$$36 \text{ ins.} = 91 \text{ cm.} \qquad 12 \text{ ft.} = 366 \text{ cm.}$$
$$15 \text{ ft.} = 457 \text{ cm.}$$

*Carpet types* Perhaps the best known names in carpeting are the woven 'Axminster' and 'Wilton' carpets—but these are not brand names. They refer to the different manufacturing techniques used to make the two types. Generally, in Axminster carpets, separate tufts of wool are inserted into the backing during manufacture, the pile being placed in position as the backing is being woven; Axminsters are generally patterned.

In Wilton carpets, all the fibres used in the pile are woven into the carpet in continuous strands; although there are patterns, Wiltons tend to be plain.

The quality of the carpet depends in each case on the amount of fibre per square inch and what the fibre consists of—i.e. wool, wool/nylon or wool/rayon blend, etc. Many woven carpets, as opposed to tufteds (*see* p. 34), made by manufacturers who belong to the British Carpet Centre are now labelled to indicate their quality and recommended usage (whether suitable for stairs, living areas, bedrooms, etc.) so look out for the British Carpet Centre label which will be a great help to you when you go to choose.

Classifications are as follows:

1. Light domestic (*e.g.* bedroom use)
2. Medium domestic use
3. General domestic and/or light contact use
4. Heavy domestic and/or medium contact use
5. Luxury domestic and/or heavy contact use

It is difficult to give an exact guide to performance on each carpet as no two households will give a similar carpet exactly the same amount of wear, and for this reason the wording on the label is in rather broad terms. It is easy to see the reason for this if you consider the difference in wear on a living room carpet between a young couple out at work all day and a mother at home with two young children. If you are able to pay a visit to the British Carpet Centre at Dorland House, 14–16 Lower Regent Street, London W1, you can look through pattern ranges and ask for advice, although you can't actually buy a carpet there—it has to be ordered through a retailer. Otherwise your local carpet salesman should be able to help. Any carpet sold with a BCC label carries a guarantee covering the weave, construction and material and is fully backed by all members of the Centre.

*Above, a room that shows a comfortable blending of new furniture with traditional carpet and accessories—ideal in a country house or cottage*

*Below, a more functional floor covering works well in this kind of room setting where the unit furniture provides valuable storage space and the room's focal point*

Tufted carpets are now very popular, the chief difference between them and the woven variety being that the pile is stitched into an already prepared backing and is not woven with it, the pile being secured by a coating of latex or other adhesive. The pile can either be looped or cut and can be either rayon, 100 per cent nylon, 100 per cent acrylic or a wool and nylon mixture. Tufteds are often self-coloured and have sculptured effects in the pattern, although new manufacturing processes have introduced more designs in a mixture of colours. In fact, when first introduced, many people considered tufteds not to be very attractive and hard wearing, but this certainly can not be said of them now. They are as versatile in use and appearance as those made by more traditional methods. Many carry a label which gives similar classification guidance to the BCC one to help you buy the right carpet for the room you have in mind, a scheme sponsored by the Tufted Carpet Manufacturers Association and the Federation of British Carpet Manufacturers (so it applies also to many woven as well as tufted carpets).

Cord carpets, which have a close, nubbly appearance, are made in a similar way to Wiltons. Hair cords are manufactured from animal fibres and are very hard wearing; rayon cords are more suitable for bedrooms.

*Carpet laying* You will probably wonder whether you can lay a new carpet yourself, or whether it would be better to call in an expert. If you are buying an expensive woven carpet, it is really better to have it professionally laid, but it is not too difficult to lay a tufted carpet or carpet tiles yourself. Some shops provide a free fitting service if you buy your carpets from them, or they may offer a service for which you pay a fee. When ordering, take a scale drawing of your room, with measurements, to the shop and the salesman will help you to work out the most economical way of ordering. This can be very useful if the room is an odd shape, and could save you money.

Always make sure when laying a stair carpet that the direction of the pile lies down the stairs, never the other way, or you will not get such good wear. You should allow an extra two feet on length so that the carpet can be moved once or twice a year to even the wear. Stairpads should be taken two inches or so over the nose of each stair tread.

*Hard floorings* The cost of hard floorings varies enormously, from the cheapest vinyl tiles to such exotic materials as marble or slate. In between comes a wide choice of cork, linoleum, wood block, rubber, hardwood, clay tiles, quarry tiles, composition block, and so on.

Many factors will influence your choice of hard flooring —whether you are intending to move again in the not-too-distant future, whether your accommodation is rented,

what you are prepared to do in the way of maintenance, and your ideas on decoration. Obviously, you will not want to spend too much money on short-term accommodation.

As with carpets, the cheapest flooring is not always the most economical in the long run—particularly if you want it to last for some time and retain its attractive appearance. Good quality vinyl tiles or slate, for instance, will keep their looks for years and work out cheaper in the end than low-priced thermoplastic tiling which has to be replaced after a comparatively short time. The following table will give you a very general indication of flooring properties, bearing in mind that there can be variations within the different categories.

| Material | Wear resistance | Warmth | Quietness |
|---|---|---|---|
| Timber (softwood/hardwood, board, block, strip), plywood, chipboard | Hardwoods very good to fair Others, fair to poor | Very good | Fair |
| Linoleum | Good | Good | Good |
| Cork tiles | Good | Very good | Very good |
| Vinyl asbestos tile | Good | Fair | Fair |
| PVC sheet, etc. | Very good to fair | Good | Very good |
| Rubber | Very good to fair | Good | Very good |
| Stone | Very good to poor | Very poor | Very poor |
| Ceramics | Very good to good | Very poor | Very poor |
| Concrete | Very good to fair | Very poor | Very poor |

**Non-slipperiness (when dry)**

| | |
|---|---|
| Timber | Good–very good |
| Linoleum | Good |
| Cork | Very good |
| Vinyl asbestos | Good |
| PVC sheet, etc. | Good |
| Rubber | Very good |
| Stone | Fair ⎫ |
| Ceramics | Fair ⎬ can be bought with non-slip finishes |
| Concrete | Fair ⎭ |

*Kitchen flooring* A kitchen floor should, ideally, be easy to clean, tough, non-slip, quiet, resilient, warm, attractive to look at and be able to stand up to such hazards as heat, spills of oil, water and fat, abrasion, chipping and cracking. Alas, there appears to be no flooring which will completely fulfil all these requirements, and what you choose depends very much on your priorities.

With most women, ease of cleaning would come high on the list, with durability and looks a close second. It is also important that a kitchen floor is not slippery for one rushes round at high speed in moments of stress with the cooking and, if the kitchen is large, children often play there too.

If your kitchen has a suspended floor—that is timber boards laid on floor joists—as it may if you live in a flat or older type of house, you will have to use a special paper underlay beneath vinyl sheet or thin tiles, as mentioned before. You will not, of course, be able to put down a floor of quarry or ceramic tiles on a suspended floor as movement in the boards would make them crack. Solid floors have no such restriction although they must, of course, be level and free from damp before any type of flooring is laid on them.

Linoleum, PVC sheet or tiles are a popular choice for kitchens as they are not expensive, are easily laid and can be changed if you decide to go in for a different colour scheme later on. Cork tiles with a vinyl finish or sealant are also becoming increasingly used; they have an attractive warm appearance and look particularly nice if continued into an adjoining living or dining room.

*Living/dining room flooring*  In its way, the living room floor will have as much to put up with as the kitchen. It may have to cope with spilled coffee, drinks and food, as well as resist sparks from cigarettes, dirt, grit, mud and any debris carried in on shoes and animal paws; and it should be tough enough to stand up to the constant tramping of many feet. This is why it is essential to buy a strong flooring (or carpet).

Wood strip or woodblock mosaics always look good and are easy to maintain. It is possible, too, to combine these with carpet, taking the wood flooring over the 'corridor' areas of the room—that is the parts which are most walked through—and insetting the carpet to cover the sitting areas so that the two floor coverings are level.

Good quality vinyl flooring can also be used and some handsome border tiles are now produced which, when used in conjunction with plain tiles, give a most sophisticated effect. Provided the room is well heated, there is no reason why it should be cold—and if psychologically it seems so, it is simple to add a few textured rugs. The room's aspect and choice of furnishing colours can make a difference too.

*Bathroom flooring*  This must, of course, be easy to clean and PVC tiles or sheet, felt-backed vinyl or linoleum are all suitable. Add warmth by providing an easily-washed mat. It is a temptation when first furnishing to carpet the bathroom—it is so luxurious and cosy. This works well but it is not really practicable when children come along, particularly if the bathroom contains the lavatory too. A washable floor is a more sensible long-term buy.

## Floor Cleaning

The type of cleaning equipment you need depends on the type of floors you have, or the floor coverings you are planning for the future.

Of the two types of vacuum cleaner, the cylinder or tank kind is usually used where most of the floors are wood or other hard materials, and the upright kind, where there are more carpets. Both types have a number of attachments, brushes, nozzles and pipes that, used on the end of a long, coiled extension, give great flexibility in use. With these attachments, you can easily reach into the ceiling corners to sweep away any lurking cobwebs, get into the corners of the stair treads and upholstery, and underneath heavy pieces of furniture without having to move them.

Carpet sweepers are versatile, easy to use, light to carry and have the added advantage of taking up much less storage space. For instance, the one we show in our fitted broom cupboard, opposite page 25, the Ewbank 1200 model, has independently sprung wheels which adjust the brush height to suit any carpet thickness and will quickly and easily sweep up crumbs or dog's hairs. This model has a large capacity and a fast-action for release of the dust collected inside. The handle lowers on its supporting bar so the sweeper can be used under furniture. Ewbank sweepers are available in a choice of cheerful colours in wood, plastic or metal cases. They are guaranteed for ten years against failure due to faulty workmanship or materials.

A great time-and-space-saver in any household is a Minit mop, which has an optional six attachments besides the cellulose sponge head. Thus the same handle, used with the range of different heads, copes with every kind of cleaning and every type of floor surface in the home.

The attachments available include a washable cotton dry mop, suitable for linoleum, polished floors, surrounds or stairheads—the quick flick-round you do just before someone comes or you dash off to work in the morning.

The scrubbing brush is suitable for floor surfaces which require a rougher, tougher treatment, such as stone, concrete or tiles, and doorsteps, terraces and concrete paths. This attachment takes the backache right out of scrubbing.

The liquid polish applicator is a non-absorbent sponge which spreads polish evenly and economically, and the solid wax applicator is ideal for use with red tile polish. The floor polisher brings up the polish on any type of floor treated with either solid or liquid polish. It has a soft sponge head and a candlewick cover.

The carpet shampoo brush has a sponge which absorbs

the shampoo while the brushes in front and behind it work up the cleansing foam and lift the carpet pile, so that the foam gets below the surface of the carpet.

The last optional attachment is a soft synthetic bristle broom, easy to use and washable.

Each Minit mop comes fitted with a cellulose sponge head, ideal for all floors from brick to vinyl, set at an angle of 45 degrees, the best position for getting under furniture and fittings and for washing walls and ceilings as well as floors.

# 6. *BEDROOMS AND BATHROOM*

## Bedrooms, beds and bedding

It does not need a very high mathematical ability to work out that a third of one's life is spent in bed! So the bedroom and its central piece of furniture deserve plenty of thought and planning when you are designing your home. Apart from being a comfortable and restful room with enough space for storing clothes, spare bedding, etc., it is a place where most women can have a free hand to express their own personal taste. The majority of men seem content to leave the furnishing of the bedroom to their wives, and so long as they have enough drawer and wardrobe space for their own things, are pleased to come into a feminine and relaxing bower arranged by their womenfolk. So you should feel free to be as pretty and romantic as you wish in your furnishing.

*The bed*   A bed is an expensive item, and if you make a wrong choice you may be letting yourself in for years of discomfort for it's not an article you can take back and change or readily replace. Buying a bed is, incidentally, something you really must discuss with your husband or husband-to-be as both your sleeping habits must be taken into account.

Remember that you change your sleeping position about 20 to 40 times a night and that ideal sleep consists of a succession of complete 'cycles' each lasting about $1\frac{1}{2}$ hours. The cycle starts with deep sleep, gradually rises to light sleep, then drops back to repeat the whole process. Four, 5 or 6 cycles satisfy most people's sleep requirements, but constant interruptions caused by noise, a restless partner, too much or too little bedding or, above all, an uncomfortable bed, will ruin a night's sleep.

If the bed you buy is too soft, the spine takes up a curved rather than a straight shape; if too hard there is too much pressure on shoulders and hips with unsupported areas elsewhere. It should be firm enough for support, therefore, but not too hard. On the whole, as you can understand, heavy people need firmer beds than lightweight ones, so you may find, if your husband is hefty and you the opposite, that two single beds joined together would suit you better than a double one (you can have mattresses of different density to suit each of you), or, if the mattresses are the same density, there will not be the same tendency for you to roll towards your heavier partner.

Another point to watch is that your bed will give enough room, especially if there are two of you to share it. The bed manufacturers have taken advantage of the change to metrication to enlarge the standard size of beds, and the standard double bed is now 150 by 200 centimetres (4 feet 11 inches by 6 feet $6\frac{3}{4}$ inches) which gives about 15 per cent more sleeping area. If you are very short of space, you will be able to buy a new 'small size' double bed roughly equivalent to the old 4 foot 6 inch bed and of course even larger sizes than the new standard will be available. Generally, the bed you choose should be roughly 6 inches longer than you are. Incidentally it is now possible to buy bedding in the new sizes, too, so this should present no problem.

When you buy your bed, go to a reputable shop or store and find a helpful assistant. Don't be stampeded but take your time about choosing, and don't be coy about lying down on the bed (take your shoes off first, though)—it is the only proper test. How much should you spend on your bed? As with most other basic household goods, you get what you pay for, and if you can afford £50 or more, it will repay you in continuing comfort and length of life. Check, too, if a guarantee of any kind is offered before you buy. You needn't necessarily include a headboard in the price—spend your money on the actual bed and improvise a headboard for the time being if funds are short.

It doesn't really matter whether you choose a spring interior mattress (either open spring, continuous wire or pocketed spring) or a foam one, but do make sure from the shop that you have the correct base with it. And never, never choose a bed just because you like the pattern on the ticking!

*Bedding*   If you are furnishing your home from scratch, it is worth considering buying Continental quilts or duvets for your bed rather than conventional sheets or blankets, although being a conservative race, many of us still prefer the latter. There are many makes of Continental quilts available now in this country, some imported, with a variety of fillings from Terylene to pure duck down. These are contained in detachable sheet covers which can easily

*Continental quilt and matching bed valance with sheets and pillowcases in a plain toning material add up to a bed that is both inviting and easy to make. The fabric designs are by Mary Quant*

be taken off for washing (choose drip-dry fabrics and you won't have to iron them). Fitted undersheets and pillowcases are the only other bed linens you will need, apart from a valance.

The quilt you buy must be large enough to hang well over at each side and the bottom of the bed or you will have undignified struggles with your partner for the possession of it! Time saved in bedmaking is marvellous, as you only give the duvet a shake and lay it back on the bed, but unless you have a summer and a winter weight you may find a standard duvet too hot in summer and have to revert to a sheet and blanket during warm weather.

Sheets, blankets, eiderdowns and quilts have never been prettier or more labour-saving. Look for machine-washable wool blankets, synthetic fibre ones in glowing colours, flowered sheets in synthetic and cotton mixtures that will drip dry and need no ironing, fitted sheets in cotton or nylon to help with the chore of bedmaking—you can even buy washable electric blankets these days for your winter comfort.

While you are about it, don't buy just any old pillow, but choose the best you can afford for it has an important part to play in your bedtime comfort and it won't keep your head and neck in correct alignment if it quickly becomes lumpy and sagging. Pillows need replacing (or should not be bought) if, when plumped up, then pressed in the middle, they do not quickly regain their shape.

Fillings are generally as follows:

*Natural fillings*
Down (duck and goose)
Feathers (land or water fowl) } can be mixed in the same pillow
Latex foam (natural rubber)
*Synthetic fillings*
Plastic foam
Polyester fibre (Terylene, Dacron)

A pillow can vary in price from under £1 to well over £5, so what are you getting for your money? The quality of down and feather pillows can be judged by weight. The lighter and fatter the pillow, the better the quality. Pure down gives good, well-distributed support but pillows made from it are the most expensive.

Feather pillows are heavier and less resilient. Chicken feathers have to be artificially curled to give resilience, but water fowl feathers are naturally curved. Foam pillows, in a medium price range, give good support and are a wise buy for anyone suffering from allergies. This applies also to pillows made from Terylene and Dacron, which also give good support. Again, they are in the medium price bracket.

If you have beds to make, rather than using duvets, try this quick method devised by the manufacturers of Irish Linen sheets. They claim that, using the ordinary bed-making technique, the 'average housewife' walks about 64 miles and spends about 400 hours a year in her bed-making. Here's their suggestion.

'Stand on one side of the bed in the centre. Spread under sheet on the bed and tuck it in. Cover this with top sheet and blankets and tuck them in. Fold down. Place pillows. Cover with bedspread. Walk to foot of bed. Toss back upper sheet, blankets and bedspread. Tuck each in firmly and pull bedspread down. Walk to other side of bed facing your starting position. Tuck bedclothes well in. Fold top down. Cover with bedspread. This way you take one trip only round the bed cutting your walking to about 15 feet.'

*Bedheads* If you are addicted to reading in bed, choose a bedhead accordingly to give you a comfortable backrest. Some have built-in bedside tables to hold books, reading lamps etc. which you will, of course, need in addition to your main lighting.

*Storage space* If you are planning to live in a large old house with big bedrooms, you will not have much problem over clothes storage, etc. There are many large old wardrobes, clothes presses and chests of drawers to be found second-hand at sales and they are quite in keeping with this type of house. However, in modern houses the bedrooms tend to be very small indeed and storage is quite a problem—especially now that beds are tending to take up more room.

If you can manage to fit in a wall of built-in cupboards containing hanging space, drawers and even a dressing-table unit, it will give you considerably more space than if you had free-standing units. Although the initial outlay may be more, it will be an attractive selling point when you come to move house, and there are many designs available in whitewood which you can fit and paint yourself, thus considerably cutting the cost.

Look round and see how you can increase your storage space. Is there room under the bed for sliding locker/drawers which can be bought separately in a variety of designs? These are invaluable for storing spare bedlinen, summer clothes in winter and vice versa. If you want a kidney-shaped dressing table, consider one which gives a great deal of drawer storage space. Or see if you can build a window seat into a bay window with storage underneath.

It is worth remembering that, even if there are only two of you now, you will probably have a growing family in the next few years and in any case will certainly entertain friends for the weekend from time to time, so it may be worth having an extra washhand basin plumbed in to your bedroom, especially if it is near the bathroom so there is not a long run of pipes. There is a good selection of pretty 'vanity units' on the market, any of which would look good in the bedroom, besides giving you a small extra cupboard and helping to free that awful early morning pressure on the bathroom.

*Decoration* This is a matter of personal choice, but flowers are, of course, traditional. You could go Victorian and choose a William Morris paper, teaming it with plain richly-coloured curtains, a brass bedstead and lace lampshades. Or you could have matching wallpaper and curtain fabric with, perhaps, a cane bedhead, cane chair and louvred wardrobe. Yet again, there are many flower patterned papers or fabrics in a contemporary idiom with modern beds, accessories and furniture to go with them.

In general the colours you choose for your bedroom should be pleasant and restful, with lighting to match, so that you go to sleep relaxed and wake up to a welcome rather than a challenge. (If at all possible, place the bed at right angles to the window so that the light does not dazzle you on waking.) Pastel colours or soft rich colours with plenty of white are more likely to do this for you than, say, orange or emerald green.

## Bathroom Fittings

Here again it pays to buy good quality fittings, economising in other ways, rather than to go in for a cheap and shiny towel rail and cabinet which will quickly deteriorate in steamy heat.

The bathroom cabinet is the largest piece of 'furniture' you will need, and it is worth shopping around to find a good one. There are some very attractive and well-designed ones on the market—two of which, both by Prestige, we show in colour opposite p. 25. As you will see, the fashionable louvred look has now appeared in bathroom cabinets—one has two roomy cupboards with a recessed mirror and shelf room between. The other cabinet is an up-dated version of the old white-and-mirror cabinet—again with good proportions, plenty of storage space, adjustable shelves and this time with a locking section for pills and medicines. With children around, this is an obvious advantage. Both are in melamine laminate that is easy to clean.

A matching set of fittings by the same manufacturers—shelf, towel rail, toothglass and lavatory paper holders—looks better than a miscellaneous collection. The pieces in the smokey brown acrylic set shown in the photograph opposite p. 25 can be bought separately. Again, they would fit into any type of bathroom, by virtue of their good and simple basic design.

It is almost essential in this weight-conscious age to have a set of bathroom scales—if you haven't any, drop hints round Christmas and birthday time! Prestige make an attractive range which are guaranteed for five years.

Having bought your basics for the bathroom, you can think of colour schemes. The two suggestions shown opposite p. 25 may appeal to you—one showing the effectiveness of matching wallpaper and curtaining, the other a clever use of tiling on the wall to give textural interest as well as being practical. Wall tiles need not necessarily be ceramic ones—you can use the vinyl tiles normally sold for floors. If money is short, simply paint the walls—either a strong deep colour, teamed with plenty of white (towels and bathmat), or all white with brilliantly patterned towels, jars and bottles and bathmat. Do not be afraid to bring a plant into the bathroom—many houseplants thrive in a steamy atmosphere and can make the room look most attractive. Think of a large plant in your all-white bathroom, with towels and accessories in shades of green! Not an expensive idea to copy but very dramatic!

---

*When money is scarce, a little imagination in the decoration can compensate. Here a free-hand effect is created with sweeps of emulsion paint that transforms the spare room. Soft furnishings and the painted whitewood furniture are all plain so that they do not compete*

# The Spare Room

With all the other expenses of furnishing a home, there may not be much money left for the spare room, but bear in mind that before children come along, it will probably have to fulfil the following functions:

1. Spare bedroom
2. Study
3. Sewing/hobbies room
4. Place for storing all those things which won't fit in anywhere else!

If you can't move to a larger house when children arrive, it will have to become a nursery, then children's room, too. These are our suggestions for furnishing a reasonably-sized double room to give it maximum usefulness at all stages.

1. Plenty of storage space is essential, for it is here that you will probably want to store spare blankets, winter clothes in summer etc. A wall of built-in cupboards would be ideal as these could be taken right up to the ceiling and provide excellent 'dead storage' space at the top as well as plenty of hanging and shelf space below. If you can include in your cupboard wall a dressing table-*cum*-desk fitment, consisting of two sets of drawers with a knee-hole between and linking top surface, you will provide a doubly useful piece of furniture which will serve for your papers and any writing you have to do, dressing table for guests, and later—much later—a desk for the children's homework! There are many different systems of built-in cupboards to choose from, some unfinished so that you can paint them any colour you want, others with pleasant louvred doors, and so on. You should be able to find room in your cupboards for sewing materials and a sewing machine if you have one, and any other things you need to store, whilst still leaving room for guests' clothes or, later, baby's and children's clothes.

2. You will probably want to provide twin beds for guests, and it is not a bad idea to buy bunk beds of a simple design which at first can be used as two separate beds. It need not be obvious, if you choose carefully, that they are bunks. Then, when the room has to be used as a nursery later, they can be put together as bunks to make room for a cot, etc. Alternatively, choose a set of two beds, one of which will fold and store under the other one. The advantage of bunks is that you will be able to make extra storage space by buying lockers to fit under one bunk. They hold a surprising amount and are invaluable for children's toy storage when needed.

3. If it can possibly be fitted in, a hand-basin or vanity unit would be invaluable—you will find it a particular boon if you have to look after a baby in the room. Otherwise it is useful when guests come to stay, and for children when they occupy the room.

4. You will also need a couple of chairs—one a comfortable small bedroom chair, the other a desk or dressing-table chair, and a small chest to go between the beds as a bedside table.

In this way you will provide a room which is well furnished and has the maximum of storage space. Decorative scheme should be bright and attractive—without being too 'bedroomy'—and a soft-backed vinyl flooring with a couple of nice rugs would be very practical and not too expensive.

There is certainly a case in this room for providing duvets or Continental quilts with covers for the guests—and later for children. They are really the best answer to bunk bed making—and for making up guest beds in a hurry.

# 7. *PUTTING THE KITCHEN TOGETHER*

How many hours a day does 'the average' housewife spend working in her kitchen? If you were asked to guess at this figure on an 'off' day, you would probably say cynically, 'Oh, 8 or 9 hours, at the very least'. And if your kitchen is inadequately planned, it can certainly feel like that sometimes. But the actual figure is $3\frac{1}{2}$ hours a day, with 29 per cent of that time being spent at the kitchen sink or the working area adjacent to it.

As if we did not already know it, then, this highly significant figure puts the kitchen right on top of the priority list for careful planning and selective equipping. For you cannot afford to be uncomfortable, irritated or bored for that length of time every day, and there is no need to be.

Before you start thinking in detail about kitchen fitments, colours or gadgets, though, think about yourself and the kind of person you are, your temperament and the life you lead. For your kitchen will be your workshop and studio. There is no prototype which is absolutely ideal for every family, though of course there are certain factors which might be called ideal common denominators.

If, for instance, you see cooking and preparing meals as one of the most artistic and enjoyable of your household tasks, and have a soft spot for that old saying about the way to a man's heart, you will probably want a kitchen-*cum*-hobby room, with space to indulge your pastimes. You would need to think in terms of providing extra storage space for home-made preserves, a freezer to store the results of a day's baking, racks for cookbooks, and more herb and spice jars than you usually see in a shop at any given time.

If, by contrast, you dismiss cooking as one of the chores you have to do at least once a day, you will probably want a businesslike, efficient unit where you can rush in, do what preparation, serving and clearing away is absolutely necessary, then shut the door on it and forget it. What you would not want is an open-plan area with a kitchen and dining or living area combined. Just think, you would have to look at it all day!

Most of us, however, come somewhere between these two extremes, though we probably at times have moods which bend us in one direction or another.

To be able to plan the ideal kitchen for you, you would need to have a house built to your own specification, or to be doing a major conversion of an older house. If you are buying a speculatively built house you will, as we have seen, have relatively little say in the actual layout: the siting of the plumbing and other services will have been specified by the architect, and the builder will go on up the road putting pipes and wires in exactly the same position in every house. Take heart, however, because the standard of kitchen design in newly built houses improves all the time and is immeasurably better than it was only a few years ago. It is most unlikely that your kitchen will waste a usable inch of space. If your choice is an older house with a workable kitchen, though not exactly to your taste, you might store up your dreams for a while and then try to put them into practice when time and money become more plentiful. You might then even decide to rebuild the kitchen in another room, more conveniently situated for your own family's pattern of living.

## Working Routine

Thinking in terms of the function of a kitchen (we will come later to colour, surface properties and appliances), it is important to consider the sequence of the work done there, to establish a pattern and then, where you have the opportunity, to design the kitchen with that in mind: your own small exercise in time and motion study, in fact. It can be established that to produce a meal one goes to the storecupboard, refrigerator or freezer; the working surface; the sink (for vegetable and salad preparation and for washing-up); the cooker; the worktop again for arranging, decorating and serving the food; and the table, if the kitchen has a dining area, serving hatch or door to the dining room. This gives us a work pattern of storage—preparation—sink—cooker—further preparation—eating.

If the kitchen were a mini factory—and in this context it is—the architect and planner would design it so that there was a continuous workflow with each operation following on the one before without interruption or wasted time or effort. So it should be in a kitchen for a housewife's time is every bit as precious. Where possible, there should be a continuous surface linking the various working centres, particularly the cooker and the sink, so that hot or heavy pans can be transferred easily from one to the other. The choice of surfaces and their heat-resistant properties is obviously important in this context: *see* the table on page 47.

## The Surfaces

A few years ago it seemed to be asking the impossible that kitchens should be decorated in materials which were both practical for the unique variety of wear they have to take, and pleasant enough to live with happily ever after. Great strides have been made, however, in both aspects, and now the task is not to find a suitable material, but to choose which one you like best.

The most durable materials, naturally, are the most expensive, but they need to be used only in the limited areas where there is the likelihood of their coming into contact with water, acid, alkalis and grease.

The area above the sink, unless it is in front of a window, and around all working surfaces, should be protected for a height of at least one foot by a material with the properties of that used on the working surface itself. Indeed, a practical way is to extend the melamine or other surface upwards; alternatives are stainless steel, glass or ceramic tiles or mosaics (easier to fit on irregular surfaces), the thinner grades of vinyl, linoleum or plastic-faced hardboard. Above this 'danger-strip' the walls can be painted with a washable semi-gloss finish paint (glossy finishes encourage condensation), or covered with a washable wallpaper or vinyl wallcovering.

It is obviously essential for the ceiling to be washable; if you live in a flat with upstairs neighbours, or are yourself particularly sensitive about noise, and have a number of electrical kitchen appliances, you might decide to cover the ceiling with sound-absorbent tiles. Check that the ones you choose do not lose their acoustic properties after re-painting.

Kitchen floors need to be kind in a number of ways: kind to the feet, since you will be walking and standing there for long periods; kind to china and glass if you should drop it; kind to the housewife without the time or inclination to spend long hours scrubbing or polishing; kind to old people and children, who might slip, and kind enough to cover up the traces when there are accidental spills.

Vinyl in one of its forms—either in sheets, or tiles, which are easy to lay and can be replaced in cases of spot wear—or vinyl-covered cork have most of these properties. In the kitchen photograph opposite p. 48 we chose Vynofoam Super in Venezuela design, a small diamond pattern imitating the cosiness of rush matting, but with many more practical qualities. Other patterns have the look of woodblock flooring, Spanish or Italian tiles, marble, mosaic or slate—so you can sensibly combine both your illusions and your practical sense.

For more details about the comparative properties of suitable floor coverings, *see* page 34.

## Furniture

Where there is space to spare, free-standing units, in a warm wood such as stripped pine, with pictures hanging on the walls, look friendly and relaxing. However, this kind of layout is the least practical, since cupboards, dressers and tables have constantly to be moved for cleaning, the surfaces need polishing to keep in good condition (unless they are 'sealed'), and the working tops are not ideal for all-purpose use. And where there is a picture the space can't be used for a wall-hung cupboard.

If you have a kitchen which is an unconventional or difficult shape, or the walls are impossibly uneven, you might decide to have cupboards built in by a local joiner; or, if you have the necessary time and skill, you might like to tackle the job yourselves.

Since in its lifetime the furniture in your kitchen is likely to come in for the hardest wear of any in the house, it is vital that it is adequate for the purpose. To save time and temper, for items that are in use many times a day, it is more than usually important that drawers don't stick, catches are strong enough to deter the dog from getting at the meat, and the working surfaces are at the right height. These requirements can be taken for granted in practically every standard range of kitchen fitments.

In small flats, or where the kitchen is in a not too readily accessible part of the house, it might be necessary to choose knock-down whitewood units which come with all the component parts packed flat in a carton. These are cheap and versatile, require a minimum skill to assemble, and come complete with fixing instructions. They might be the answer, too, if you like to make a real contribution to your homemaking, but do not feel able to undertake building the units. You can choose whether to stain or lacquer them, or paint them any colour or combination of colours you choose: in other words, you can stamp your personality on a whole range of kitchen furniture in a way that the designer might never have envisaged!

For the kitchen photographed in colour opposite p. 48 we chose a range of knock-down furniture that is both adaptable and efficient. Units are based on a module measurement—a standard width and depth applied in various multiples to the whole range—which gives great flexibility and will be found suitable, in various combinations, to practically any size and shape of room.

These units, with tough hardwood framing and precision jointing, are designed for the heavy wear and tear of workaday kitchen life. The heat-resistant worktops are ¾ inch thick and include a balancer laminate underneath to avoid possible distortion. A flexible plastic sealer strip takes up minor wall irregularities—a boon even in some newly built houses, you will find. The drawers run smoothly on nylon gliders, with safety stops to ensure that they cannot be pulled out by mistake. Anyone who has accidentally pulled out a drawer full of knives, icing nozzles and biscuit cutters will commend this attention to detail.

All the doors are fully laminated on both sides, lift off for easy cleaning, and open a full 180 degrees so that every part of the cupboard is easily accessible. Rust-free pull handles running the full width of both doors and drawers mean that there are no awkward protruding handles, and door and drawer edges are laminate-protected against knocks and water penetration.

Notice the mid-way storage unit which, although only 4½ inches deep, with sliding figured glass doors and two shelves, makes full use of the gap between worktop and wall unit. It houses small items like condiments, spices, herbs and baking powders, protecting them from steam and dust. A light fitting below wall cupboards gives a glare-free light on to work surfaces and is completely unobtrusive.

Our choice of door fronts was sapele, a rich, warm colour; alternatives are walnut colour and grey tweed. All are melamine laminates, which means that the surface is practical and wipes clean. All the drawer fronts are white and the worktops a grey tweed satin-finish melamine.

This mixture of warm, white and neutral colours, we found, gave us ample opportunity to make our own colour impact in the kitchen decoration.

With a flexible range of this kind, kitchens can be practically purpose built. Units are available to take a high-level oven, and a cooking hob; there are single and double drainer stainless steel sink units, the larger one being fitted with a removable, washable cutlery tray, and open and closed corner wall units.

Items in this Debutante range, from U.B.M., are available through their builders' merchants. They come packed flat for home assembly, and most will fit into the boot of a car.

The following table gives the kitchen working heights recommended by the British Standards Institution (BS 3705). These are average recommendations, to which most kitchen furniture manufacturers now refer. If, however, you are particularly tall or short, it might be necessary to make adjustments. This may be done by means of suspended or wall-hung units, adjustable plinths or by having your units 'made to measure'.

Naturally, only the most fortunate of us will be able to buy all the equipment listed at the outset of kitchen planning. It is as well, however, to study this table for advice of the appropriate spaces to leave for appliances you hope to acquire in the future, and particularly what heights covering working surfaces need to be.

## Working Heights

| Item | Height (in inches) |
|---|---|
| Top of highest shelf for general use | maximum 70 from floor. Any space above that would be used for 'dead' storage |
| Clearance between general working level and underside of wall-hung fitments above | normally 18, to allow space for appliances |
| General worktop level | 34 |
| Table (where additional worktop) | 28 to 30 |
| Top of sink | 36 |
| Bottom of sink (inside) | 29 (if a sink deeper or shallower than 7 inches is fitted, the level of the top should be maintained) |
| Top of floor-standing appliance to go under worktop | maximum 33 |
| Top of floor-standing appliance to go under draining board | maximum 34 |
| Store for ironing board | minimum 66 |

| | Depth front to back (in inches) |
|---|---|
| Worktop (which may extend beyond floor fitments at back) | 20 and 24 |
| Floor fitments | 12, 16 and 20 |
| Wall-hung fitments | maximum 12 at bottom or 10 if clearance above worktop is less than 18 |
| Other equipment | maximum 24 |

| | Width (in inches) |
|---|---|
| Fitments | 12, 20, 24 and combinations of these figures |
| Main worktop surface | minimum 40 continuous length |
| Space for free-standing gas or electric cooker | 24, 28 and 32. Clearance of 4 inches is needed between cooker and appliance next to it unless cupboard, etc. is specially insulated |
| Space for free-standing solid fuel cooker | 30 or 40, with 4 inches clearance |

| | |
|---|---|
| Space for free-standing refrigerator | 24 or 28, with 4 inches clearance |
| Space for hot water or central heating boiler | 20 or 24, with 4 inches clearance |
| Space for built-in appliance or fitment for built-in appliance, such as cooker or refrigerator | minimum 24 |
| Space for sink and draining boards | 44, 64 or 72, with fitments below sinks and draining boards |
| Space for dishwasher | 24 or 28 |
| Space for washing machine, automatic washing machine or twin tub washing machine | 32 |
| Space for tumbler drier or drying cabinet | 28 |
| Space for rubbish container | 16 |
| Space for ironing board | minimum 18 |
| Space for space heater if required | no floor space—recommended wall fixing |

### Clear space

| | |
|---|---|
| Width of working space between faces of equipment (the 'passage' in the middle of a kitchen with equipment on both sides) | minimum 48 |

N.B. At the time of writing, the subject of working heights is under discussion during the revision of standards in line with the metrication programme. Some manufacturers are working to the old standard for the top of the sink as 36 inches, or 900mm; some use 34 inches, or 850mm, while other manufacturers offer both heights. Some kitchen equipment is made to a regular width of 21 inches, (533mm) or multiples of that measurement.

## Working Surfaces

Since there is no single material which is ideal for the multitude of tasks it has to perform, a worktop will have to be either a compromise, a material which copes reasonably efficiently most of the time, or a combination of materials used together providing different areas for different purposes.

Consider the number of jobs you might do on a single stretch of worktop, and you will see how difficult the choice is. You will be measuring ingredients, sifting (fine powder everywhere), chopping, cutting, sawing, rolling pastry (cool surface needed), standing hot pans, arranging flowers, cooling jam, mending toys, wrapping parcels, sorting laundry. . . . The list is endless.

Perhaps the ideal is to have a continuous working surface in one of the most satisfactory of materials, with inset panels of, say, end-grain sycamore for chopping, and asbestos insulated board, stainless steel or ceramic mosaics for standing hot pans and tins from the cooker.

In older houses, no plumb line would give comforting assurance of the levels of walls and floors and here it is perhaps a good idea either to have cupboards and other fitments purpose built, or to choose one of the range of units designed so that a purpose-made top can be fitted and trimmed to the undulations of the kitchen walls. In this way, too, you have a wider choice of materials and yet effect a saving by being able to buy factory-made units.

Generally, melamine laminates are most suitable for general kitchen use. They resist a certain amount of heat, though you need to have a trivet or other insulated stand for oven-hot pans. They come in an attractive range of patterns and good colours, can be supplied coved up the wall at the back for easy wiping (no dust in the hard right-angle) and with a drip stop along the front.

The following table shows the comparative qualities of a number of the different surfaces available.

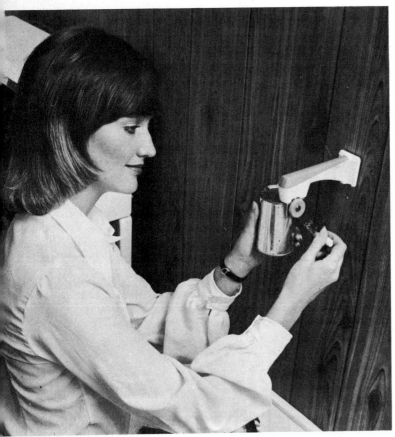

*Wall can-openers, in the same way as general working surfaces, should be at a comfortable height for the user, as well as being over a working surface and within range of the waste bin*

| Surface for working tops | Thickness needed for 2ft. (600mm.) span | Special finish | Properties | Do-it-yourself Cost |
|---|---|---|---|---|
| HARDWOOD: Choose from beech, birch, maple, sycamore (for chopping block) and teak. Used solid, timber may split. Advisable to use thick-cut or laminate veneers about $\frac{1}{8}$-in. thick, on chipboard base | $\frac{3}{4}$in. solid timber. For veneers, back with $\frac{3}{4}$in. chipboard | First 4 can be rubbed with olive oil, teak with teak oil, to give greater resistance to heat marks. All may be finished to advantage with polyurethane lacquer | Easy to clean; durable; fair resistance to heat, good resistance to stains; easy to repair: sections can be cut from either solid timber or veneer and replaced | Medium. Obtainable from leading timber merchants |
| SOFTWOOD: Usually pine, solid, or faced blockboard, chosen for its natural appearance. Not suitable for heavy-duty areas unless finished with polyurethane lacquer or similar, and well looked after | As for hardwoods | If not given a protected finish, can be scrubbed | Easy to clean when lacquered; poor otherwise. Reasonably durable; fair resistance to heat, good resistance to stains only when given protective covering. Easy to repair | Cheap from D-I-Y shops and timber merchants |
| PLASTIC: Formica or similar melamine laminates as durable general-purpose surface | $\frac{3}{4}$in. chipboard with balancing veneer for Formica when worktop is not firmly fixed | None | Easy to clean; durable; good resistance to heat and stains. Difficult to repair. A whole length needs replacing if damaged | Medium |
| HARDBOARD: Oil-tempered grade, $\frac{1}{8}$in. Can have coloured plastic surface similar to Formica, but less durable | Glue on to $\frac{3}{4}$in. chipboard, treated as for veneers | Polyurethane lacquer unless surfaced with plastics | Easy to clean; durable if plastic-coated, otherwise fair. Reasonable resistance to heat and good resistance to stains. Difficult to repair, especially when plastic-coated | Cheap from D-I-Y shops and timber merchants |
| PLYWOOD: Usually tight-grained birch ply. Must be resin-bonded and waterproof | $\frac{5}{8}$in. solid | As for hardboard | Easy to clean; durable; resistant to stains and reasonably resistant to heat; difficult to repair | Cheap from D-I-Y shops |
| CERAMIC TILES AND MOSAIC: Useful near cookers. Must be jointed with epoxy resin which gives a tough, hygienic joint. Decorative mosaics are useful for filling in small areas | $\frac{1}{2}$in. chipboard or $\frac{5}{8}$in. asbestos insulating board in areas of very high heat | None | Easy to clean; durable; well resistant to stains and heat. Easy to repair: damaged tiles can be lifted out and replaced | Medium-to-expensive |
| METAL: Stainless steel, stain- and scratch-resistant grade. For areas where hot pans are put down and for drainers | 15 gauge | None | Easy to clean; durable; good stain- and heat- resistance. Difficult to repair | Expensive |

The above table is adapted from the one in *Kitchens*, a Design Centre Publication, by John Prizeman.

## Storage

Every kitchen should be planned with adequate space to store dry goods, fresh fruit and vegetables, other perishable foods which need ventilation or a refrigerator, and frozen food, whether it is to be home-grown or bought in bulk. The amount of space needed for each of these categories will depend on the size of your family, where you live, the accessibility of the shops, whether you want to shop once a week or every day, whether you grow your own fruit and vegetables, how much you plan to entertain and, obvious though it sounds, the type of food you like.

Your storage will be at different levels, with some floor-standing units, some wall-mounted and some at waist level. Unless you see bending and stretching as part of your keep-fit programme, you will want to site food, linen, utensils and cleaning materials near the areas where they will be used. This, too, may seem to go without saying, but one of us, who has an old farmhouse kitchen, has to admit to keeping kitchen knives in a drawer 19 feet away from the working surface where they were used. It took an exhausted weekend guest to point out the error of this particular way!

It is practically impossible to plan your food storage so cleverly that you will never have to turn out a whole cupboard to reach a tin of baking powder, or get out your step-stool to get to a packet of cornflakes. If you make a note of inconveniences of this kind, gradually a pattern will emerge whereby you keep the items constantly in use roughly at waist height and near the front of the shelves, the lesser-used articles towards the back or higher or lower, and the reserve items further still from reach.

Dry foods can be stored in their packets or boxes, but since these might become damp and the contents deteriorate, it is better to empty them into glass bottles, plastic boxes or metal drums. Glass containers have the advantage that it is easier to see when supplies are getting low, but are, of course, breakable. It is not necessary to buy a range of expensive ones: save coffee or other commodity jars and you can build up your own matching set. Dried herbs can be kept in glass jars, too, but only in small quantities at a time, since both colour and aroma deteriorate with long exposure to light.

Vegetables should be stored in the special compartment in the refrigerator or in a rack, allowing ventilation all round and with a tray underneath to collect the dirt. Some vegetables, too, particularly potatoes, suffer change of colour and flavour if left in the light, so these should be kept in a rack in a cupboard. Since vegetables need washing either before or in the course of preparation, it will be most convenient to store them near the sink unit.

The decision to have or not to have a refrigerator will be taken largely on economic grounds; the question will surely not be 'if' but 'when'. For a refrigerator is in every way the most efficient larder you can have. Every millimetre of space is used, with shallow racks in the doors to take the small items, and shelves at different distances apart and of different widths.

The official recommendation for ventilated larder space is a minimum of 4 square feet, and newly designed kitchens will have this provision. Where space is not severely limited though, we cannot emphasise too much the convenience of having more than the minimum storage space.

Home freezers, as well as refrigerators, come into the category of storage and we discuss on pages 62-63 what a freezer can do for you in terms of saving time and money. However remote such a purchase might seem at the present time, do not rule it out, for we have never yet met a freezer owner who could contemplate life without one.

## Cleaning Materials

You will soon accumulate a motley collection of cleaning materials, some of which will be in daily or weekly use (see the advice on page 91) and others which will be needed only once or twice a year. Here again, as with the storage of food, a pattern should be devised whereby you can most easily reach the things in frequent use, and be prepared for a little more effort now and again to get to the others.

To demonstrate this point, we took a standard, narrow broom cupboard, already fitted with recessed shelves, and planned it inch by inch to hold the household cleaning materials to be found in most kitchens. The cupboard which you can see in the colour photograph opposite page 25, stands 78 inches high, is 21 inches deep and 21 inches wide.

Taking a leaf from the book of the refrigerator designers, we fitted shallow, plastic-covered racks to the inside of the door, positioning them so that they did not impinge on the shelves when the doors were closed, and used them to store shoe-cleaning materials, small tins of copper and silver cleaners and so on. The hooks accommodated a teapot-spout brush and pot scourer—untidy if left on the draining board and as elusive as needles in a haystack if put away in a drawer—dusters, floorcloths and scouring cloths. Hanging these items is the most hygienic way of storing them, as air can circulate round them. A soap dish holds a large spare bar of soap at the ready for the time when someone shouts that there isn't any anywhere.

On the top shelf, two plastic boxes hold nails and screws, wall plugs and all the other bits and pieces the man of the house needs but never seems able to find. There, too, right at the front where you can quickly lay hands on them, are spare electric light bulbs, a large household box of matches, too cumbersome for even the most absent-minded to put in

*The warm sapele colour of the melamine surfaces on the Debutante range of furniture and the copper cladding on the stainless steel cookware inspire a homely, efficient kitchen. Non-stick bakeware, Colour Clad pressure cooker and weighing scales with metric equivalents make light work of cooking. The working surfaces are grey tweed melamine laminate and the floor vinyl sheeting is in a rush matting pattern.*

The right kitchen equipment will lighten any task. The Skyline ham slicer (above) and the carving set (below, left) are tailor made for their jobs. The Hi-dome Colour Clad pressure cooker (below, right) saves hours of cooking time and can provide nourishing, economic meals.

his pocket, and, just below, a torch and box of candles, ready for the inevitable power cut or fuse crisis. This area is reserved for practical-minded pessimists!

Behind the candles are decorating tools and materials and the remains of tins of paint, which should never be thrown away when a decorating job is finished. You might not rue the day until the cat scratches the kitchen door or a piece of furniture is pushed into a wall—then you will.

Spring clips (which come, fitted, with the cupboard) hold the Ewbank carpet sweeper in place and secure the Minit mop and floor polisher handle. The attachments for these items are on a shelf behind.

The plastic-covered wire basket holds all the cleaning materials you will normally want as you go around the house—rubber gloves, scouring powder, polish, scrubbing brush, dusters and all-purpose cloths. It is rather like having your suitcase packed ready to go away: when the time comes, you have everything you need ready to hand.

The accessibility of any piece of equipment in the kitchen determines to a large extent the amount it will be used, and whether or not it will pay its way. For practically any household task is quicker performed by hand than with a tool that is under a pile of jam jars at the back of a cupboard at floor level.

In an air-conditioned kitchen, or in a country area where dirt and dust are not a problem, open shelves, racks, hooks and slots can be provided for all the items in regular use. A workmanlike row of good-looking equipment is convenient for the housewife, encouraging to visitors, and decorative. In towns, however, it is advisable to keep all but the items in daily use in cupboards or drawers. This will save you from having to wash them even when they have not been used, and will prevent deterioration.

Small every-day equipment, like knives, spoons, peelers and so on are best stored in a shallow drawer fitted with compartments. Most standard kitchen units are supplied with at least one of these. The knives should always be put away with the handles nearest the front, all in one direction, so that there is no danger of your grasping one by the blade. Larger knives can be slotted into a rack on the inside of a cupboard door, as long as they are out of reach of children. The more rounded kitchen tools, such as whisks and beaters, need a deeper drawer compartment, and a complete set of kitchen tools—which you will be almost sure to need every day—can be hung conveniently on a rack over a working surface.

Bakeware, bowls, basins, measuring jugs and similar items should be stacked where possible and stored neatly on shelves in a cupboard—again near the area where they will be used. If your kitchen units or other cupboards have adjustable shelves, so much the better, for then you can 'tailor' them to your requirements.

In kitchens with no dust problem, saucepans can be stored on a shelf above the working surface or, if there is space, on a free-standing, tiered rack for saucepans and lids. Where there are young children, or boisterous animals, though, free-standing, lightweight units are not recommended. In urban kitchens, it is advisable to store pans away. Some kitchen units have a drawer deep enough for pans and lids to be stored, conveniently at waist level, or they can be neatly stacked in a cupboard. Hinged cabinet doors can be fitted with racks to take pans—though this of course considerably reduces the available storage space of the cupboard when the door shuts.

## Heating

Your kitchen must always be warm and cosy. Nothing is more depressing on a cold winter's morning than to come downstairs to a chilly kitchen to start the day. The effect to aim at is that of a kitchen which has a solid fuel cooker—and indeed where this is the case, there will not usually be any need for a further heat source.

There will probably not be room for a radiator. If your kitchen is well planned, every scrap of wall space will be making some other useful contribution to time and labour saving.

Underfloor heating is often the solution, albeit an expensive one, with hot water in copper pipes, electric cables or warm air ducts for concrete floors, or electric cables specially fitted under timber floors.

Wall-mounted heaters have their place in a kitchen; a thermostatically controlled fan heater, which can also be used for cooling the room in summer, is worth considering. In a small room, a wall-mounted infra-red heater might be adequate, but as only a limited area in front of the appliance is heated, you might find yourself toasting when you were cutting up the meat and freezing when icing the cake.

A supply of constant hot water is essential in any kitchen, and one of the provisions for which you can apply for a local authority improvement grant.

The method you choose to heat your water will vary according to your heating system (*see* chapter 3) and the size and type of your house and kitchen. It can be by means of a gas, oil-fired or solid-fuel boiler, or by an electric immersion heater. In a small kitchen, a wall-mounted gas water heater—which needs a flue to the outside—or an electric appliance would be adequate. They all provide instant hot water at the turn of a tap, perhaps one of the greatest of all the advantages the modern housewife enjoys.

## Ventilation

Efficient ventilation is essential in any kitchen, and there is no need and no excuse to put up with windows curtained with rivulets of condensation, or a room penetrated by the less pleasant cooking aromas.

Ideally, steam and smells from the cooker should be extracted by fan through a hood above it and conveyed by a duct through an outside wall, or the roof in a bungalow or top-storey flat.

Extractor fans, to be thoroughly efficient, should be able to extract 18,000 cubic feet per hour, be easily accessible for cleaning, and have a shutter to close when they are not in use. The closer the hood can be to the cooker, the more efficient it will be, since less steam and smells will escape around the sides.

On conventional cookers, a hood cannot be lower than two feet above the hobs, because of the necessity to reach underneath it to the pans at the back. In split-level cookers, where the hobs can be designed in a single row along the back of a heat-resistant working surface, the hood can be at the minimum height that allows pans to be moved easily and safely beneath it—about 18 inches.

If it is not possible to fit an extractor fan and hood over the cooker (because of the inaccessibility of an outside wall, or in rented property where such modification might not be permitted) a window extractor unit can be used as an alternative. In this case, it is important to check with the retailer that the fan can cope with the cubic footage of your kitchen before buying. One with too low a capacity will leave you wondering whether the thing is working at all, and with too powerful a motor, it will take away not only the smells but the heat, and leave you and your kitchen shivering.

# 8. *YOUR KITCHEN EQUIPMENT*

To make the best use of all your equipment, such as electric kettle, food mixer, liquidiser, iron, vacuum cleaner, floor polisher, you must give careful thought to the siting of the power points. Go through a work routine—where you would stand or sit to iron, make a cake, grind the coffee—before you decide on the position of each source of supply. A little thinking at this stage can save you hours of frustration and wasted time later on, when cables might not reach or equipment be too large or too high to stand on the only working surface near the power outlet.

## Electrical Fittings

It is estimated that a fully equipped kitchen needs at least 10 universal 13-amp socket outlets (a complete 30-amp ring main circuit, in fact), one 30-amp cooker outlet, or two if the cooker and hobs are separated, and a 20-amp water heater outlet. Waste disposal units need a separate 13-amp outlet and should be earth-bonded to metal sink and taps. The lighting circuit will have to allow for the general, directional and cupboard lighting you will need.

It is most unlikely that you will be able to equip your kitchen at first with all the appliances you need, but when the electrical circuits are being installed, it is as well to allow spare fuse ways for the future. In a speculatively built house, this would probably be an 'extra' to the purchase price.

Where possible, plan your socket outlets in pairs, since these cost very little more than single outlets to install. In this way, you will not have to wait until the electric kettle has boiled before you can make the toast, or finish whisking the eggs before you can grind the coffee.

The Electricity Board, incidentally, quotes about £5 to add a power point to an existing circuit. If you plan to add extra ones yourself, take professional advice about the circuit's capacity.

All the plugs should be appropriately fused; details of loading will be given in the instruction manual supplied with each appliance. If you are likely to forget to switch off a piece of equipment when you have to go to the telephone or the front door—perhaps when you are ironing—fit a neon indicator light and then train yourself to be aware of it and what it means. As with tying a knot in your handkerchief, it will be useless unless you remember what it is there for, and what you should do about it.

## Washing Machines

Many experts on kitchen planning advocate a separate room for laundry or, failing that, the installation of a household sink or a washing machine in the bathroom, if it is big enough.

This point of view does have merit because the high humidity of a kitchen makes it about the most unsuitable room in the house for drying washing. Added to that, racks of laundry close to a cooker constitute a fire risk, and act like a sponge to cooking smells. We have not yet met a husband who favours shirts scented with cabbage!

On the other hand, it is convenient to have laundry equipment in the kitchen, especially if you have a non-automatic washing machine. You can be getting on with other jobs and turn your attention to the machine or the dryer when necessary.

A washing machine will probably be high on the list of requirements for most newly-married couples. There are three main types of domestic washing machine: twin-tub, semi-automatic and automatic, with a considerable difference in prices.

**Twin-tub machines** are loaded from the top and wash, rinse and spin dry from $3\frac{1}{2}$ to 7 pounds dry weight of washing. They need attention because the laundry has to be manually transferred from the wash to the spin dry tub. This is where it is an advantage to have the machine in the kitchen and attend to it when needed. Top-loading, of course, means that if the machine is stored under a fixed working surface it will have to be pulled forward when in use.

**Semi-automatic machines** are loaded from the front and can cope with heavier loads—from $6\frac{1}{2}$ to 9 pounds of laundry at a time. As the term implies, they need to be controlled manually, but the laundry does not have to be handled as with twin-tub models.

**Automatic machines,** more expensive than the other types, have the advantage that they can be loaded, the required washing programme set, and then left to run the full cycle. They have, therefore, a great advantage: you can go to bed or go out and leave the laundry to take care of itself—a considerable aid to a sense of freedom from the kitchen sink! Larger models will take up to 10 pounds dry weight of washing.

Most models have up to eight different programmes, including one for pre-wash rinsing of exceptionally soiled garments—football gear, for instance—blankets, delicate fabrics, whites, coloureds, woollens, drip-dry garments and for extra spin drying.

A few automatic machines have an extra heat drying cycle which will tumble dry the wash to any pre-set degree of dryness, giving the same ready-to-iron properties that are offered by the drying machines in launderettes.

Separate heated dryers are available for home use and have the advantage over the washer and heated dryer unit combined in that you can be washing one load and drying another. The combined machines can perform only one task at a time.

Tumble dryers, front loaded, can be pre-set for any degree of dryness and take from 6 to 9 pounds of washing at a time. They give good results, leaving the fabrics almost crease-free. This type of unit usually needs a duct through to an outside wall and so its positioning in the kitchen is critical.

Less sophisticated than these are airer dryers which can be housed under a worktop or in a cupboard. Washing is hung on racks on much the same principle as standing a clothes airer in front of the fire—but infinitely safer—and the released moisture is captured within the cabinet.

Spin driers, which are needed only if you do not have a washing machine, because spin drying is part of every washer cycle, leave the laundry part damp, and not usually dry enough to iron.

## Ironing

Ironing machines are useful when there are large amounts of laundry to be done regularly, but will not normally be considered worth the outlay in a small family, at least while funds are limited.

The two types, flat-bed and rotary, deal efficiently with straightforward items, but an ironing board and conventional iron will still be needed for the smaller, more fiddly items. The flat-bed type is simple to use but slower than the rotary which, however, needs more skill in operation.

Since many broom cupboards are not large enough to store ironing-boards (the one we used in our photograph opposite page 25 was not), this leaves the problem of what to do with the board when it is not in use. In a two-storey house, there is usually a cupboard under the stairs, an invaluable no-man's-land that houses everything of awkward size and shape from an old school trunk to the vacuum cleaner, the ironing board to camping equipment.

In flats and bungalows, there is often a cloaks cupboard in the hall; perhaps the ironing board could be a tenant in there!

Built-in ironing boards, which fold away flat, against a wall or into a cupboard, overcome the storage problem, though they do have the slight disadvantage that they cannot usually be adjusted to heights suitable for use when both sitting and standing. However, if you already know which position you prefer for ironing, you can have the board built in to hinge down to that level.

Before buying an electric iron, test the weight of it in the shop by holding it, balancing it and pretending to use it. Different models vary quite considerably. The choice of the right one for you can turn tedious and tiring work into a reasonably light task. Steam irons, useful for dry work where you are advised to 'press under a damp cloth' —notably when pressing hand-made or other woollen garments—need distilled water to fill them. It is advisable to know this before the iron becomes faulty, and you turn to the instruction manual. You should, therefore, keep a supply of distilled water in a plastic bottle in the kitchen, ready to hand when you need it.

Clothes airers in plastic-covered metal combine maximum amount of airing space with the minimum amount of storage space needed when the airer is folded away. Where washing is not allowed to be hung out in the garden, you can usually stand a portable clothes airer outside. Clothes lines in plastic are easier to wipe down and keep clean than rope ones; the umbrella-type of airers, some of which have a sunshade to make double use of the stand, are designed to take a great deal of washing and occupy a limited space, but they do occupy it all the time as most models cannot be put out of the way.

## Cookers

Before choosing a cooker you must decide which of the two main fuels you will use—one or other, or both. Advances in the application of both fuels have largely evened out earlier differences.

Gas hobs give the maximum required heat immediately on ignition and, a point which is comforting to some users, the heat is visible; but some of the high-speed electric hobs can boil faster than gas ones. Any kind of saucepan can be used with gas, but flat-bottomed pans are best on electric. Both gas and electric hobs can have thermostatic simmer controls, and both are available now with the new easily-cleaned flat glass hobs. In more conventional models, gas hobs are usually easier to clean than most electric, since they can be removed and washed.

Still on the subject of cleaning—and for some housewives oven cleaning is, or was, the biggest bogey of all— make sure you look at some of the electric ovens with a self-cleaning device. They can be switched on to a very high heat, with the door sealed against accidental opening, and the residue burned off. In other ovens, both gas and electric, side, top and bottom panels, as well as the shelves, are removable. However, you will still find it an advantage to wipe down an oven with a damp cloth while it is warm to minimise the task later. One couple we know take it in turns to clean the oven thoroughly, inside and out, before serving the Sunday lunch, which has to wait in the warming drawer, but we think this is carrying pride too far.

Gas ovens give a hotter temperature at the top of the oven, cooler lower down, which is why some recipes specify on which shelf to put your cake or puddings. In electric ovens, the heat is even throughout; they normally take longer to reach the pre-selected temperature than gas—a point which, in both cases, must be borne in mind in food preparation. You can save time by switching on the oven before the food is ready to put in. Some electric ovens are available now with a 'grill booster' which cuts down the warming-up time.

Although one-piece cookers give the maximum possible hob and oven capacity in a given floor area, it is a decided advantage to have a split-level cooking unit if space and money permit. This way, you can use a combination of fuels.

One advantage of having split-level cookers is that you can fix the oven at working height, the right level for you, eliminating the need to stoop with hot and heavy dishes and trays. Hobs can be arranged in a long, straight line, rather than the usual square formation, and have a heat-resistant working surface alongside or in front.

Solid-fuel type cookers, a feature of country kitchens, can now be fired by gas or oil instead, which makes them cleaner to use and cuts out the riddling, emptying and filling routine; they are all self-cleaning.

## Dishwasher

Most families take about $1\frac{1}{2}$ hours a day to wash-up and clear away after meals—quite considerable when you calculate how much time, by comparison, is actually spent eating.

With a dishwasher, this time can be cut considerably, though not altogether, for time must be allowed to rinse plates and dishes of excess food and load and unload the machine. However, dishwashers earn their keep in terms of space, for china, glass and cutlery can be stored in them, as in a cupboard, until needed at the next mealtime.

Usually, a dishwasher will give more efficient results than washing-up, leaving both flatware and cutlery shining and free from stains, and will cope easily with all but the most baked-on dirt—such as the roasting tin, for example.

Without doubt, the use of a dishwasher would cut down considerably on breakages in a household where cup handles have a habit of coming off in the hands of willing helpers. But they are not recommended for articles susceptible to high temperatures and the use of strong detergents (*see* table on p. 54).

It is not economical to use a dishwasher after every meal, unless of course it is full. Save the washing-up—out of sight in the machine, not stacked on the draining board—until a full load can be put through. Small models which stand on top or fit under a standard working top take six place settings—that is, three meals for a family of two, or two meals for three people. This loading, of course, does not take account of all the basins, bowls, whisks and other items that might have been used in the preparation of the meals. These might well qualify for a separate washing programme of their own.

Since dishwasher models vary in the type of loading racks they offer, you should check before buying one that it will accommodate the type of articles you are most likely to want to wash in it. For instance, some very deep fruit bowls, or very tall glasses will not fit into some machine layouts. It would be a pity to discover this amid the excitement of using your kitchen 'fairy godmother' for the very first time.

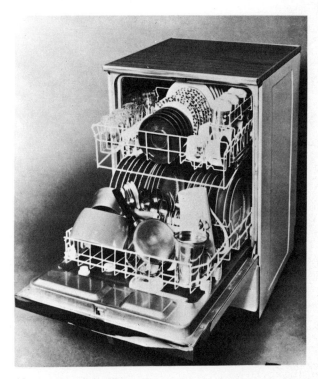

*Many modern dishwashers will cope with pots and pans in the same load as china and glasses. This one is stacked and ready to go—saving someone a long washing-up session*

Most machines are permanently plumbed in, with the waste water hose either fixed to discharge into a sink, or sited so that it can be hooked over the side of the sink when in use. This is perfectly satisfactory, as long as you are not absent-minded enough to switch on the machine without first placing the hose in position. If you do, the amount of water discharged, after a cycle consisting of pre-rinse, two detergent washes and between two and five rinses, will give you more trouble than a week's washing-up put together.

```
DO NOT PUT IN A DISHWASHER:
    Over-glaze china
    Gold leaf-decorated antiques
    Thin-stemmed glasses
    Bone-handled cutlery
    Any thermoplastics
    Any light plastics such as
        food boxes
        beakers
        bowls
    Any items with non-stick finishes
    Stainless steel dishes
```

## Waste Disposal

In this age of convenience foods and pre-packaged goods of every kind, the disposal of containers is an increasing problem. In the home, we should grind or burn our refuse to leave as little as possible to be collected by the authorities.

The most efficient—and most expensive—equipment is an electric or gas incinerator. These machines burn refuse to a fine powder which can then be used as a garden fertiliser—but this by-product cannot really be put up as a justification for the initial outlay. Some oil-fired central heating boilers are designed to take refuse and some solid-fuel cookers will take a limited amount—though your ability to burn waste in this way will depend on whether or not you live in a Smoke Control Zone.

A rubbish chute fitted near the sink, to discharge waste through the wall into a large container below, is easy for the housewife, for you do not have to empty bins from the kitchen into dustbins. But it leaves the whole of the waste to be collected by the authorities. Do be sure that such a chute is burglar-proof, for you could be providing the unscrupulous with an ever-open door to your home.

A waste disposal unit fitted to the sink deals with a great deal of messy kitchen waste, but not all. It disposes of small amounts of paper and card and all food refuse including bones. (It is far safer to feed bones to the waste disposer than to leave them around where a cat can get at them.)

But it cannot cope with metal, rags or string which would clog up the works, plastics, cans, china or glass, or large amounts of paper or card.

There are two types of waste disposal units, which have the same capacity of materials. One, the continuous feed type, where the machine is always open and is controlled by a switch; the other, marginally safer where there are small children around, is the batch-feed type. Waste is fed in and then a safety plug inserted which, when turned, starts and stops the machine. This gives you the opportunity to snatch back any item, such as a ring or hairclip, that has got there by mistake.

Only stainless steel or plastic sinks can be converted to take a waste disposer, though new sinks of any kind can be fitted with one. They require a special $3\frac{1}{2}$-inch diameter waste outlet. If the unit is fitted to the only sink in the kitchen, there should be a separate waste outlet, so that if it should jam, the sink is still functional in the normal way. Cold water is used to wash down these units: hot water melts grease and fat and clogs up the pipes.

Even with a waste disposal unit, you will need a bin in the kitchen. Plastic pedal bins in good subtle colours blend well with decoration schemes and, used with an inner liner, are easy to keep clean. If you have a garden, you will find it worthwhile to make a compost heap for use as a general fertiliser. To do this, have a separate waste bin and save coffee grounds and tea leaves, fruit and vegetable peelings and dead flowers—they will all help to make your garden grow.

If you live in a rural area, you might be asked by the local authority to divide your refuse into separate categories—tins, paper and compostable materials, and provide appropriate containers for each. Many authorities now provide large black plastic bags for refuse collection—which makes lighter work for the dustman and has obvious hygiene advantages.

When choosing a dustbin, remember that plastic ones will not take hot ashes; a galvanised bin with a rubber lid will take ashes and will not disturb the neighbours as would the cacophonous metal-on-metal of an all-galvanised one.

## Sinks

Think of an average day in the life of a kitchen sink and the variety of calls that are made upon it, and you will see that it is asking practically the impossible to expect a single sink to cope. You can manage with one sink, but there is bound to be time wasted while one member of the family waits for another to finish preparing vegetables, washing dusters, filling a kettle or flower vase, or washing-up. A double sink halves this frustration and increases the efficiency of the kitchen.

Right-handed people work from right to left, and would use the right-hand sink for washing up, the left-hand one for rinsing; the right-hand draining board for dirty dishes, the left-hand one for draining.

In this case, the right-hand sink would need to be only about 6 inches deep and could then, ideally, have a recess beneath it so that you could sit down to the work. It has been estimated that your duties at and around the sink account for 29 per cent of your time in the kitchen. Particularly if you have no dishwasher, it is important to have a shallow sink for washing-up, so that to reach into it you do not have to bend too far below the right working height for you.

If you have a separate sink for rinsing, there is practically no need for drying up, since plates immersed or sprayed with hot water will dry on a rack quickly and without smears. With only one sink, the handling of crockery and cutlery involved makes it almost as quick to dry with a cloth.

Although they are more expensive, stainless steel sinks have practical advantages over fireclay or enamelled cast-iron, as anyone who has banged a galvanised bucket against an enamelled sink will testify. Plastic sinks are resilient but need very careful use.

Choose swivel mixer taps, particularly with a double sink unit. This way, you avoid ever having to put your hands under icy cold or scalding hot water.

## Buying Appliances

As one advertisement for a brand of washing machines said, 'The only real difference between washing machines is what happens when they go wrong'. With roughly 124 million electrical appliances in use in the United Kingdom, and with each one likely to go wrong once every three years, that statement has a great deal of significance.

There are few really bad pieces of equipment on sale, but it follows that the more sophisticated machines become, the more there is that can fail and cause you temporary inconvenience. Manufacturers differ widely in their attitude and approach to after-sales service. Some firms have service centres throughout the country, to repair articles both in and out of guarantee, and others leave the retailer to sort out the problems and arrange for repairs.

With built-in items, like washing machines, refrigerators, dishwashers and cookers, it is vital to know what the servicing arrangements are; where the service centre or capable retailer is, and how quickly they are likely to come in response to your call.

If you live in the country, the main advantage one piece of equipment has over another might very well be the simple fact that one manufacturer has a servicing operation in your nearest town and the other has not. Remember that time costs money; if an engineer has to travel miles to your house, you will pay as much for that as for the time he actually spends on the repair.

When you are buying an appliance, be relentless in the number of questions you ask the retailer or the electricity or gas board representative. You need not feel embarrassed; your kitchen appliances will represent some of the biggest single items of expenditure after your home itself and a motor-car, and you want to make sure that your capital is wisely spent.

Ask how long the appliance is meant to last, given 'average' wear and tear, and assuming that you will use it according to the manufacturer's instructions. This way, you will be able to work out the rate of depreciation and how much it will cost you over the years.

Ask how long the manufacturer intends to continue making spare parts; there is nothing more infuriating than to be told that a model is out-of-date and it is no longer possible to get replacement parts.

If possible, ask for a demonstration, and be sure to get an instruction manual. However much you try to concentrate on what you are told and shown in the showroom, something is bound to crop up that you had not thought of asking.

Find out what there is to go wrong—after all, the retailer will have been dealing with the complaints of other customers and must know what they involve—and how much the repairs are likely to cost. How long do they take? And will you be able to have an estimate before committing yourself? If an appliance breaks down in several years' time this will help you decide whether it is worth having it repaired, or better to buy a new one.

It is obviously not possible to give complete and up-to-date details of repair charges for all manufacturers. One big company making large electrical appliances, which has a network of service centres, quotes £3·50 for the first thirty minutes (including travelling time) and 50p for every further fifteen minutes. Thus, for a job which took the engineer two hours to reach you, put the matter right, and get back to his depot, you would pay £6·50, plus the cost of any spare parts needed.

## Small Electrical Equipment

When buying portable equipment, you need to ask much the same questions as for the larger items. Ask for a demonstration if it can be arranged, and check on any points not covered in the handbook. For instance, if you have never used a steam iron before, you might not know that it has to be filled with distilled water; with an electric kettle, that it has to be kept free of 'fur' inside to maintain maximum efficiency, and that a packet of de-scaler will help; with a coffee grinder, that you must never allow water to come into contact with the rotating paddles and, with some models, that you have to hold the lid in place if you are not to shower the kitchen with that aromatic powder.

If something goes wrong with a portable appliance, your first step is to take it back to the shop or electricity board showroom where it was bought. If it was a present, or you have moved away from the district where you bought it, take it to the nearest stockist of that make, telling him what the trouble is and when the appliance was bought. If it is still under guarantee, take the card with you. If the stockist does not undertake repairs and cannot recommend you to someone who does, you might have to return the appliance to the manufacturer, at your own expense. Be sure to include a letter with it, explaining just what is wrong.

You can take out an insurance policy to cover the mechanical failure of an appliance. One policy, for example, offers cover for all servicing costs, no matter how many times the machine might go wrong in a year, and a free maintenance check at the end of each year. This is significant, because if appliances are checked regularly, and minor repairs carried out, they are less likely to give trouble later on.

A policy of this kind is cost-related to the equipment, roughly £5 a year for a medium-sized refrigerator and £11 a year for a washing machine, with a cover charge of an extra £1·25 for each call the engineer is asked to make.

Before deciding to take out a policy, assess the information you have gleaned from the retailer, and ask anyone you know who has a similar appliance. You might find that it is cheaper to take the risk of an occasional breakdown than to commit yourself to this annual outgoing. After all, you might be one of the lucky ones and have an automatic washing machine, electric food mixer or iron that will give you completely trouble-free service for ten years or more. If so, it is likely to be due at least in part to the care you took in choosing it.

## Saucepans

With the right type of cookware, which quickly and efficiently conducts heat, is safe to handle, easy to keep clean, your cooking will be a real pleasure and your pans become like tried and trusted friends.

Pots and pans have to withstand a great deal of hard wear and tear, and extremes both of heat and type of contents, so it is vitally important that you choose them with care, either when you are buying them yourself or making up your wedding present list.

Pans in constant use will be lifted from the working surface, to the drainer, to the hob, to a heat-resistant sur-face or stand, to the sink, and back to their cupboard or shelf again. Sometimes they will be full of hot foods, some-times, especially the larger capacity ones, they will be heavy; sometimes you will be in a hurry, or might be careless, so it is important to choose pans that will not break, chip, flake or peel and which 'handle' comfortably.

Although you will probably have chosen a cooker with at least one high-speed boiling ring, you will not want to have to use it all the time because it is wasteful of fuel. It is essential, therefore, to choose pans which conduct heat evenly over the whole of the base, without building up 'hot spots', and which, once heated, keep the pan and its contents at an even temperature on a low heat.

We bore all these points in mind when choosing the pans to show in the kitchen photographed in colour opposite page 48. They are from the Prestige Cookware 8600 series, made from stainless steel in which a combination of various minerals, including a high proportion of nickel, has been added to the basic metal, iron. Since stainless steel is a strong material it will not damage in daily use; it is also the least affected by chemical reaction in contact with food, from oil and fats to acids.

Stainless steel alone is not a good conductor of heat, but these pans have a 'sandwich' or radiant heat core of mild steel between two layers of stainless steel. This gives the advantages of having three pans, one inside the other: the outer and inner layers with the qualities of stainless steel, whilst the middle one ensures the best possible use of the heat.

These pans should never be put on a very high heat. Once the pan and its contents are heated through, an even temperature is maintained with a low heat source. The ones we chose have a copper cladding on the base, which spreads the heat even faster to the enclosed radiant heat core.

With safety in the kitchen of such vital importance, we looked for pans with a wide base, shallow enough to resist knocking over. These have short stubby handles, another safety measure; they overlap with one another less on top of the cooker and are less likely to be knocked against and toppled over. Combined with the extra stability of the shallow shape, this makes them particularly suitable where children are likely to be able to reach them.

The cover for each pan has a curled edge to match the base and forms a vapour seal. If a cover starts to 'rattle' during cooking, it means that the heat has been left too high and is a reminder that these pans function at their best on a low heat.

Separate covers are available for frying pans in many cookware ranges. Using one in the early stages of frying saves splattering fat over the stove and surrounding areas and cuts down cleaning later on. It means, too, that the pan can be used as a skillet for slow cooking, steaming fish, braising vegetables, making risotto and so on, or for re-heating foods which need no more than gentle warming through. Covering a frying pan ensures that the heat is 'trapped' and the food cooks right through to the centre without getting overbrown on the outside, yet still allows it to become crisp.

Looking ahead to after-sales service, it is comforting to know that Prestige cookware, for instance, is guaranteed for ten years against faulty materials or workmanship, and that knobs and handles are replaceable, available from stockists throughout the country.

Those who like kitchenware with a definite personality might be inspired by the Prestige French Provincial style saucepans, frying pans, etc., with teak handles and slightly rounded bodies, or the subtle orange-and-green design on white of the enamelled Country Kitchen range. Each has an associated range of household accessories. Available in one or both of the ranges are step stools, spice racks, rolling pin, apron, tea towels, place mats, oven gloves, cheese and chopping boards and clip-on note pads.

*Fireproof earthenware*  Other types of cookware you might like to consider are fireproof earthenware casseroles and baking dishes which are ovenproof and in some cases can be used on top of the stove over direct heat. The latter is a common way of using fireproof earthenware on the Continent, but in this country many people feel rather nervous of doing so. However, there is no danger of the earthenware cracking if a few simple precautions are taken.

The main thing to remember, both cooking in the oven or on top of the stove, is to heat up the casserole or dish slowly at first and keep the heat low and steady throughout the cooking process. Earthenware retains the heat and it is a good idea to check or reduce heat, when the right stage of cooking has been reached, by placing a special mat under the pot and over the flame on the cooker top. Never add cold liquid to a casserole containing hot fat, meat, etc. and don't wash up the dish until it has completely cooled down. In fact, avoid 'shock' treatment caused either by heating up the cold pot or cooling the hot one down too quickly.

Don't worry if the glaze on your earthenware pot appears 'crazed' when liquid is poured into it. It does not mean a fault in the glaze, but merely that it will expand when hot.

*Vitreous enamel pans*  Vitreous or porcelain enamel pans or casseroles always have a clean smart appearance and may now be bought in an attractive range of colours and patterns. Basically, vitreous enamel is glass (opaque, not transparent) and it is applied to the metal of the pan by firing. On cooling, it sets to a hard smooth finish which is durable, heat- and scratch-resistant and colourfast. It is easy to clean, provided the pan is washed up fairly soon after being used, so that food is not allowed to dry on. Some abrasive cleaners are not good for vitreous enamel articles, and if in doubt it is as well to check with the Vitreous Enamel Development Council of 28 Welbeck Street, London W1M 7PG, who can send you a list of recommended cleaners. In recent years thinner, more damage-resistant enamel finishes have been developed and good quality vitreous enamel is now much less liable to damage than in the early days of manufacture.

*Aluminium pans*  Aluminium saucepans, if properly looked after and of good basic quality, will give years of service. Before using for the first time, wash in hot soapy water, rinse and dry. Frying pans should be 'proved' by melting a small piece of fat in the pan, removing it from the heat and sprinkling with kitchen salt. Rub hard with a piece of kitchen towel, then empty the salt away and wipe with a clean cloth. This will make the pan ready for general frying, but if you later wish to use the pan for omelets, you should repeat the 'proving' or they will stick.

For general washing up, use a liquid detergent and a brush or fine steel wool pad (not a copper scouring pad or scouring powder). Rinse in hot water after washing, and wipe completely dry before storing.

If a pan develops black stains inside from boiling eggs, steaming puddings, etc., they can easily be removed by boiling apple or rhubarb trimmings in it. Never use soda for cleaning aluminium pans, and remember to stir food with a wooden spoon rather than a metal implement.

*Cast iron pans*  These pans, generally in the form of frying or omelet pans, are normally lightly coated with grease before leaving the factory to prevent them from rusting. To remove this coating, warm the pan, then wash it in hot soapy water and dry completely. Heat a little olive oil in the pan until it is quite hot, then tilt the pan so that the oil runs and covers the sides. Allow the oil to cool, pour it off and wipe the pan with paper towel before storing. Do not wash the pan after every use, but wipe out with kitchen paper. If you do have to wash it, make sure it is completely dried, then brush lightly with olive oil before putting away.

*Non-stick pans*  Many pans are now available with non-stick finishes and are particularly acceptable in the form of milk saucepans and frying pans. Very often the non-stick coating is PTFE (or polytetrafluoroethylene!). Among the trade names you will find on the saucepan label are Fluon, Teflon, etc. The coating resists all common chemicals and solvents, and withstands high temperatures. Avoid using sharp metal kitchen implements in a non-stick pan; keep to plastic or wooden spoons, spatulas, etc., and do not scour when washing; simply use hot water and a soft cloth. Other non-stick finishes are also available.

# Knives

Few pieces of equipment are more often used than a knife —or, rather, a variety of knives. You need knives to cut, chop or slice, peel and pare, trim or bone. But as every good cook knows, you cannot do all these jobs with one tool. There is a right knife for every job, with the right length and shape of blade (*see* page 60).

A selection of three or four knives would give a new cook a good start. You will need a paring or utility knife for dealing with vegetables; a French cook's knife with a 6- or 8-inch blade for general use; a carving knife and a bread knife. Later, or as additional presents, you will want to add more special-purpose knives for cheese, preparing grapefruit (the curved, rounded edge of this knife makes it almost invaluable for obtaining perfect results), a spreader, a ham slicer with a long thin blade so that you can slice cold meats evenly and thinly, and, if you have a home freezer, a frozen food knife.

To choose the best knife for the job, and to keep them in the best working order, it is as well to understand the differences between plain hollow-ground and scalloped-edge blades.

If you look at an ordinary knife you will see that the blade thickens from the cutting edge to the back; this is necessary to give strength with flexibility. However, this means that each time you sharpen a knife you are trying to put an edge on to an increasing 'thickness' of blade. The purpose of the hollow-ground edge is to 'scoop' out the blade to a certain depth, so that this thinner edge can be more finely sharpened and, on resharpening, the razor-like property retained.

These blades need to be 'touched-up' at intervals to maintain maximum efficiency. Most housewives will find the easiest way to do this is to use a rotary knife sharpener which can be wall-mounted or kept in a drawer near a working surface. The wheels are set to the correct angle to fit a hollow-ground blade. All you need to do is to draw the blade through three or four times to obtain a perfect cutting edge once more. This must be done regularly. It is a mistake to allow a knife blade to get dull before trying to correct it.

Scalloped edge knives are the equivalent in cutlery of the carpenter's saw. Some brands, such as Prestige, have blades that are first hollow-ground and then scallop-ground. This technique gives the blade a double efficiency —the 'bite' of a serrated edge to start off the cutting whilst protecting the fine hollow-ground edge so that it retains its sharpness.

For general kitchen use, the scalloped edge may give better results for cutting through food with tough outer surfaces, such as bread, tomatoes, lemons and root vegetables. The plain hollow-ground edge is usually preferred for chopping herbs, dicing vegetables, cutting up meat and poultry and for carving at the table.

# Tools and Gadgets

A good selection of kitchen tools and gadgets is essential to make light work of your everyday tasks, for there is no doubt that the right ones will save time and temper.

Do not be persuaded by the guile of some demonstrators selling a tool that is claimed to do practically every job in half the time. There are very few such versatile gadgets and you will find that, as in the case of knives, you will be far better served by one designed for each specific job.

Potato peelers are almost as personal as your handwriting. One which is like an extension of the right hand of one cook will make another seem awkward and clumsy. If you have the chance, try out the ones your relations and friends use and then decide which is the right one for you. It might be the Skyline 'Speed' peeler, with a sharp swivel blade, ideal for potatoes, with points to take out the eyes and, used rhythmically, practically sure to take the peel off an apple in one long, satisfying spiral. The handle of this tool has a four-cutter grid for slicing beans. Another Skyline peeler has a hardwood handle bound with cord for a non-slip grip—comfortably solid to hold; and there is one which reverses to an apple corer.

But, as we said, it is a matter of choice. One of us admits to taking her favourite peeler whenever she goes to stay with friends for the weekend; and usually manages to convert them to using one like it.

Whisks and beaters have a variety of different tasks to perform in the kitchen. You will need a rotary beater with rust-resistant wings, of the type we chose for our 'model kitchen', and, for jobs where you need a hand free to hold the basin or to add one of the ingredients gradually, a one-hand beater; lastly, specially for whipping cream, a special whip with a spring action.

As your interest in cookery grows, and you discover a special liking for one form or another, you will build up your stock of the appropriate gadgets. If you like pastry-making and cake decorating, you will want a set of biscuit and pastry cutters—metal ones are best, because they have a sharper cutting edge and do not 'drag' the edges of the dough; a pastry trimmer and crimper to give neat, decorative edges to your work and a pastry brush to cover the surface of your tarts and pies quickly and hygienically with egg.

---

*Cooking becomes easier and quicker with the right tools. Here are the Skyline superchrome 2200 series set of ladle, potato masher, three-prong fork, spatula, measuring spoon, batter whip and omelet turner, on a hanging rack. The enamelled hardwood handles are available in a choice of colours*

To make your first attempts at Christmas and birthday cakes look like anything but first attempts, you will need a basic set of icing nozzles. Look for a set with an icing pipe and four decorative nozzles to give you a variety of shell and star patterns.

On the subject of decorative finishes, put a selection of gadgets on your wedding or Christmas tree present list, things like a butter curler, food baller, egg slicer and tomato slicer will give you, faster than anything, a reputation as a cook who flatters her guests by taking time and trouble over the preparation of her food. The secret is, of course, that with all these gadgets at your side, you will take far less time and trouble than they think!

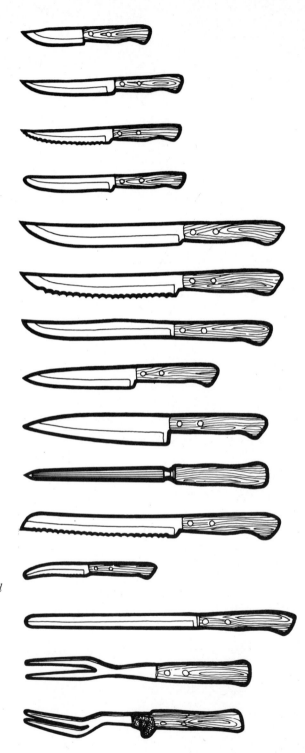

*Prestige 600 series of Super Sharp Cutlery with bonded wood handles. From the top, they are:*
*Paring Knife*
*Utility Knife*
*Utility Knife (scalloped edge)*
*Steak Knife*
*Carving Knife*
*Carving Knife (scalloped edge)*
*Steak Slicer*
*French Cook's Knife*
*French Cook's Knife (large)*
*Sharpening Steel*
*Bread Knife*
*Grapefruit Knife*
*Ham Slicer*
*Carving Fork*
*Carving Fork (with built-in guard and knife sharpener)*

# 9. *ORGANISING YOUR TIME*

Let's assume that you now have the ideal kitchen (or will have—for even if it is not yet quite a reality you know how to plan and buy towards it for the future). How then are you going to make the best possible use of the kitchen, and of your time. This section contains a few hints to help you.

When you clean the house (*see* Chapter 12) a good deal of repetitive work is involved and you can, to a certain extent, 'switch off' your mind and think about other things as you go round with duster and mop. But your activities in the kitchen are a good deal more creative and involve a certain amount of emotional satisfaction, too. In Anglo-Saxon times, the woman of the house or hall was known as the 'loaf-giver', and the preparation and offering of food to the family and friends is still enjoyed by most women in the same way. Being a good cook, thinking out your meals and cooking skilfully is satisfying as an intellectual exercise and, with reliable equipment to help, you should not take up too much of your working time in the week.

## Planning the Shopping

If you can set aside a few minutes every week to plan meals for the next seven days and jot down your shopping requirements, you will find it time well spent. We once knew a young housewife who, carried away by enthusiasm, planned her meals for a year ahead on a card-index system, but this is going too far! You need not, of course, stick rigidly to your plan if on going to the shops you find that some particular product is especially cheap and good that week—simply substitute it for one of your planned items.

Assuming that you have a refrigerator with a compartment for storing frozen foods (but not a home freezer—*see* p. 62), what would be a reasonably time-saving way to organise your shopping and cooking?

If you have transport, it is obviously sensible to try to buy the bulk of your food once a week with, perhaps, a further minor shopping expedition at the weekend for a joint and any other odd items which are needed. Stock up on household basics such as cleaning materials, pet foods, etc. once a month if you have room to store them, so that

they needn't always figure on the weekly list. Obviously you will also keep basic tins and packets in the store cupboard in case of emergency (*see* p. 95).

## Time-saving Cookery

If you are out at work, you will probably not be at home for tea-type meals except at the weekends. However, these are much more enjoyable if they include home-made scones and cakes, so an evening's baking towards the end of the week is a good idea if you can manage it. Once-a-week baking, even if you are at home and have more leisure, is more economical of time and cooker heating than several small sessions.

If you are batch baking it helps tremendously to have really well-designed and efficient bakeware. Prestige, for instance, make a non-stick range which will not rust and which, with its special silicone glaze, will keep its performance and appearance through years of use. (Some of this ware is shown in the kitchen photograph opposite p. 48). For many mixtures such as pastry, biscuits, rock cakes, gingerbreads, Madeira cakes, etc. (that is, rubbed-in and melted mixtures) there is no need to grease or line the pans—the cakes etc. will turn out perfectly and cleanly.

If you are making fatless mixtures, such as whipped sponges or meringues, you need oil only slightly. As this particular bakeware has anodised surfaces it is particularly efficient and you can cut down quite considerably on cooking time—perhaps as much as 15–25 minutes for a large fruit cake.

If you use anodised bakeware for successive batches, washing up is kept to a minimum. Normally at the end of use you need only wipe the pans with a damp cloth or wash under the hot tap (but don't use soap, detergent or particularly washing soda as they can have a harmful effect on the anodising). Only if jam, fat, etc. is baked on to the pans must you soak them for a few minutes before wiping clean.

On baking day, plan to make a mixture of scones, sweet and savoury, and different kinds of pastry and cakes, some of which will have to be eaten soon after baking, and others which will, if stored in airtight tins or in the refrigerator, be fresh to eat at the end of the week. (You would, for instance, eat a light sponge as soon as possible after baking, but a rich fruit cake would taste even better after a few days' keeping.) It is a good idea to store some uncooked pastry in the refrigerator for use later in the week as pie crust, tarts, etc.

It is also a saving in time, energy and cooker heat to cook several days' meals at one time. For instance:

| Day | Cooking | Meal |
|---|---|---|
| Sunday | Weekend roast joint Casserole Baking Ham | Hot roast |
| Monday | — | Re-heated Casserole |
| Tuesday | — | Cold ham with salad |
| Wednesday | Shepherd's Pie Roast Chicken | Shepherd's Pie |
| Thursday | — | Reheated chicken in gravy |
| Friday | — | Chicken omelet or risotto |
| Saturday | Fish or cheese dish | Fish or cheese dish |

As you can see, a little forethought will soon help you to develop your own menu plans and short cuts—and give you more time to experiment with new dishes among the tried old favourites.

## Home Freezing

If you begin to develop the batch-cooking mentality in your week-by-week cooking, your mind will undoubtedly at some stage turn to the subject of home freezers. In recent years, more and more people have realised what a tremendous convenience and saving in time and money they can be.

The basic principle of deep freezing is to lower the temperature of food, either cooked or uncooked, down to −18 degrees C (O degrees F) or even lower, and to keep it at that temperature so that bacteria growth in the food is almost completely stopped. It is important that this freezing process takes place quickly, because if food is frozen too slowly it can deteriorate and when thawed it may bleed or drip and have an unattractive appearance.

Very large quantities of food cannot be frozen all at once from cool. It has to be done in batches, and generally speaking, it is possible to freeze roughly 3 pounds of food per cubic foot of freezer space every six hours or so.

The two main types of freezer are the front-opening upright type and the top-opening chest type. For the modern kitchen where space is at a premium, the upright type usually fits in better and is, in fact, rather more convenient for packing in and taking out food. However, it tends to 'spill out' more cold air when the doors are

*One of the larger freezers now available—a 16-cubic-foot chest model that has a counter-balanced lid and interior light*

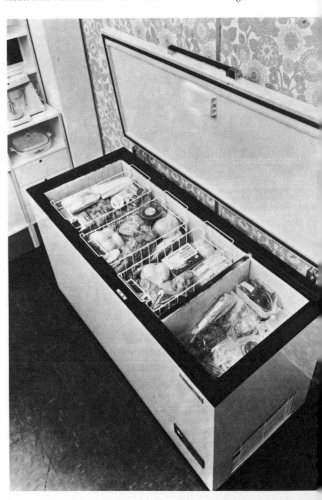

opened than the chest type. Chest freezers tend to be slightly cheaper to buy and freeze food rather more quickly. They offer, too, a wider choice. A freezer could, if necessary, go in a garage if suitably dry and cool, in a cupboard under the stairs if sufficiently ventilated, or in a box room. Always check, incidentally, if you are small and the chest freezer you are thinking of buying is large, that you can reach down to the bottom of it without taking a header inside.

Sizes vary from about 3 cubic feet capacity to 12 cubic feet or even larger, and it may be a temptation if the family is small to buy the lower size. However, all the freezer owners we have ever spoken to advise buying the largest freezer you can afford and accommodate. They say it is a greater economy in the end, both for storing vegetables and meat when they are cheap and for putting in meals you have pre-cooked yourself and for keeping bulk (and therefore cheaper) packs of ready-frozen foods.

There's a good deal of 'know-how' involved in making the best possible use of a freezer—in planning, preparing, ordering for and packing it to suit the very individual requirements of your own family, and it is advisable to read a good book on the subject before you begin. We recommend some on page 100.

## Freezer Questions and Answers

Here are some of the questions people frequently ask when they are thinking of buying a home freezer—and the answers.

Q. Can I freeze food in the star compartment of my refrigerator?
A. No. The frozen food compartment is intended only for storing ready-frozen foods up to three months, according to the star rating.
Q. How much does it cost to run a home freezer?
A. Freezers use about two units of electricity per cubic foot per week. The cost will, of course, depend on the charges for electricity in your district.
Q. Can I put cooked food direct from the oven into the freezer in order to cool it down more quickly?
A. No. Hot foods should be cooled down as much as possible before freezing.
Q. How long can I keep food in my freezer?
A. The length of time varies for different foods—and again it is advisable to consult a detailed list in a specialist book on freezing. For instance, cooked casseroles, stews, etc. will keep for two months, whilst uncooked beef and lamb will do so for a year. If food is stored longer than the recommended times, the flavour and quality will deteriorate. Thus you can see that it is particularly important to label each package in the freezer with not only the name of the contents but also the date frozen.

Q. Is de-frosting a freezer an awful chore?
A. No, it is not a difficult job and needs doing only once or twice a year in the case of chest freezers and two or three times a year for upright models. Choose a time when stocks in the freezer are low, say, before the summer fruit and vegetable season, or when stocks of meat are nearly finished. In each case, follow the manufacturers' instructions. There are now freezers on the market which have automatic defrosting, so enquire when you are buying your particular model.
Q. What happens if the freezer breaks down or there is an electricity power cut?
A. Whatever you do, leave the freezer closed until a few hours after the electricity starts coming through again, if the cut is only of short duration. The food will stay in perfect condition for at least six hours, and the more food there is in the cabinet the longer it will keep frozen. If other electrical appliances in the house are working and it is the freezer itself which has broken down, ring for servicing at once and keep the cabinet closed until you obtain the agent's advice. You can insure with certain firms against loss of frozen food in freezers.

## Pressure Cookery

If you have used, or eaten meals cooked in, a pressure cooker, you are probably convinced already of their usefulness and effectiveness. But for those of you who haven't, this section will, we hope, help you to make up your mind about pressure cookery.

Pressure cookers are generally of the flat top or dome variety, either pan or casserole type, and vary in size from about 7 to 16 pints capacity. Have a look at the versatile Prestige range which varies in interior finish (some models have a 'Teflon' non-stick coating), exterior finish (see the attractive colour clad outside of the cooker shown opposite page 48) and size, so that large or small families can be catered for.

*What is 'pressure cooking'?* Most women are interested mainly in results, rather than how they are achieved, and there certainly seems to be an element of magic in the way a pressure cooker, correctly used, can transform a tough cut of meat into a succulent stew in a matter of minutes rather than hours! However, the principle is really quite simple.

Under normal kitchen conditions, cooking liquids boil at 212 degrees Fahrenheit or 100 degrees Centigrade and you can go on boiling food for hours without this temperature being raised. But by increasing the atmospheric pressure—that is, confining the steam from cooking liquids in a steam-tight container in which pressure can safely be built up—the temperature will rise and steam will be forced through the food, causing it to become cooked and tender in a comparatively short time. This saves fuel as well as all those precious minutes waiting for something to be ready. The flavour of the food is sealed in and many vitamins are retained by the rapid cooking, even though they are subject to more intense heat. In fact, less Vitamin B1 is destroyed and a good deal more Vitamin C is retained by pressure cooking.

With the special trivet and separators supplied you can, of course, cook several different foods at the same time, thus preparing a whole meal together. As the food is cooked in steam, the flavours will not mix.

As well as cooking such obvious things as meat and vegetables, you can make steamed and other types of pudding and even such delicacies as cake and fruit loaf! Sterilising baby's bottles, making pet foods, preserving, blanching vegetables for home freezing, bottling fruit and vegetables and sterilising such items as bandages can also be done in it.

*Cooking Times* How much time is it possible to save by using a pressure cooker? Here are a few examples of actual cooking times, once preliminary preparations and pressure cooking stages have taken place.

| | |
|---|---|
| Green vegetables and root vegetables sliced and cut small | Most take 4–5 minutes |
| Dried vegetables | 15–30 minutes |
| Stock made from bones, root vegetables, etc. | 30–45 minutes |
| Vegetable soup | 5 minutes |
| Leek and potato soup | 8 minutes |
| Chicken soup from carcass and vegetables | 7 minutes per pound plus 5 minutes |
| Fish | From 3 minutes for plaice fillets to 12 minutes for salmon |
| Beef stew | 15–20 minutes |
| Savoury mince | 7 minutes |
| Curries | 12–20 minutes |
| Stuffed hearts | 30 minutes |
| Liver | 4 minutes |
| Pot-roasted beef | 12–15 minutes per pound |
| Boiled mutton | 15–18 minutes per pound |
| Chicken with peas and rice (meal for 4 people) | 5 minutes |

The advantages of owning a pressure cooker are obvious if you are a working wife, but it is a piece of equipment which can extend its range of uses when eventually you are living at home with a small family. If you enjoy camping and caravanning holidays, the pressure cooker can go with you too—it would be a great addition to the usual two-burner Calor gas cooker or primus stove.

*The French Provincial range of stainless steel cookware comprises four covered saucepans, a milk saucepan, frying pan and chip pan with basket and cover. The satin-finish stainless steel tools are from a set of six on a hanging rack. There is a wide range of matching textiles and other items with this fresh and attractive pattern, shown here on the glazed pottery rolling pin, heat-resistant table mats and white linen tea towel.*

*Dinner for two could look something like this. The stainless steel tableware is Old Hall and the glassware is Bridge Crystal.*

# 10. CHINA, GLASS AND CUTLERY

It is generally advisable—particularly if you are a breaker by nature—not to use the best glasses and wedding-present dinner service all the time in the rush and scurry of a working week. This does not mean to say that the pottery plates and mugs and the glass you relax with in the evening need be coarse and cheap-looking—far from it. There are many attractive designs available at a reasonable price and, provided you wash it with care and dry it well, you can give yourself the luxury of using your well-chosen and well-designed cutlery all the time.

## China

Although you may be tempted into buying different patterned china or earthenware for best use, for breakfast, tea and dinner sets, it is really most practical to go in for a dinner service and tea and coffee set in the same pattern. This has the advantage of economy—for the pieces are interchangeable for different meals—and the convenience that your mats, tablecloths and napkins can be chosen to match. Make sure that the design you choose will not date too much and that you can be reasonably certain you will both like it still in a year's time! If it has associated small pieces, besides the main ones, such as honey jars, small occasional dishes in different shapes, and so on, so much the better. They can be collected for Christmas and birthday presents and can enrich your set immensely.

When choosing, check that the pattern will be in production for a number of years to come and that pieces can be bought separately. In fact, it is not a bad idea to buy as a special insurance a plate, cup and saucer, etc. extra in each size, put them away and forget about them.

People are often confused about the difference between earthenware and china. There is a basic difference between the two. Earthenware is made from a mixture of different clays, ground stone and flint. The colours and patterns are fixed into the glaze so that they are completely permanent. But earthenware is more easily chipped and broken than china and once the glaze has been damaged, it is porous underneath.

Bone china is made from china clay, china stone and up to 50 per cent of calcined bone ash. It is finer than earthenware, pure white basically and is translucent when held up to the light. The decoration, however, unless under the glaze or fused into it, may not be so resistant. Sometimes colour and gilding is applied over the glaze (particularly in older china) so that the china must be handled and washed with care. A new manufacturing process has recently produced a range of English Translucent China which is very much cheaper than the traditional bone china and combines its delicate appearance with its strength and durability. Traditional and modern patterns are available.

Another point to bear in mind when choosing your china is how it will look when food is put on it. This is very easy to forget, for one can be so carried away by the beauty of a pattern that one fails to imagine it gradually emerging from beneath a helping of meat, potatoes and vegetables. The combination may not be very attractive!

If you take care of your best china it should last you for many years. Here are a few simple hints.

1. Never expose it to sudden extremes of heat and cold. Heat alone should not cause it to crack if applied very gradually, but sudden heat, or sudden cold, can do so. If you want to warm plates, stand them on a warming rack above the cooker or heat in a bowl of warm (not boiling) water. If you put them in the oven to warm, start them off at cold and increase the heat very gradually. Never expose china to the direct heat of a naked flame.

2. Always wash china separately from cutlery, pans and glasses. Keep a rubber mat in the bottom of the sink and wipe off all left-overs with a piece of kitchen towel. Never scrape these off with a knife or you might well damage the glaze. Wash the china in hand-hot water and use a mild detergent. Rinse in hot water and place in a plastic-coated rack, finally polishing with a clean, dry cloth.

3. If you have tea or coffee stains in cups or tea or coffee pots, clean off with borax and rinse thoroughly. A baby's bottle brush is useful for cleaning inside spouts.

4. If you intend to use a dishwasher, enquire before buying your china whether it can be washed in one of these, and if there are special instructions. Also check

that the shape of the pieces allows for them being fitted in. We know of one unfortunate person who bought a dishwasher and then found that none of her 'best' set plates would fit in!

5. When storing the china, avoid piling the plates too high and slip a piece of kitchen towel between each to protect the glazed surface. Never slide one plate out from under a pile of plates, particularly if there is no padding between. Hang cups on curved, not square, hooks.

## Glassware

Having chosen your china, you can go on to select glass and cutlery patterns, for you probably will want to relate them. If you are not choosing them all together, it is a good idea to take a separate plate with you when you go to look at patterns. It will help you make up your mind when you have narrowed down to two or three favourite designs.

Some styles of tableware just will not blend happily together—chunky pottery teamed with delicately cut crystal and traditionally patterned silver would look odd, to say the least. Make sure that the overall style is right, and will look good in the dining room and on the table you eventually plan to set.

Again, it is wise to keep a few glasses for every day. Although they may not be expensive and have the quality of your best ones, they can still be well shaped and pleasant to hold. At the same time, start collecting sets of best glasses. Many of the charming designs from the Bridge crystal range would match in well with china in a simple modern design or with a more traditional elaborate pattern. Glasses such as these, which are made from fine full lead crystal—crystal which has a high percentage of lead oxide, giving the glass its transparency and sparkle—take time, care and craftsmanship to produce. The lasting pleasure of owning a set makes them well worth saving for.

Start with a set of tumblers which will serve for water, soft drinks or spirits, a set of wine glasses and a set of sherry glasses. The others can be added as you can afford them or kind friends give them to you. Many people are worried about the right type of glass in which to serve different kinds of drinks, so we give you a diagram to help you. However, etiquette is not so strict on this point as it used to be, and you are unlikely to be censured because you don't serve claret in the correct glass or because sherry glasses have to serve if you are offering liqueurs!

To make your glassware sparkle, wash in warm water and washing-up liquid (always separate from other dishes and cutlery), then rinse in hot water containing a little borax. Wash the glasses one at a time—don't dump them in the sink all together as crystal could scratch crystal— and dry with a lint-free cloth, giving a final polish with a

*From left to right, hock, champagne, brandy, claret, port and sherry glasses*

soft tissue. Never stack your good glasses one inside the other but place side by side and upside down on a shelf, not touching one another.

If by any chance two glasses do become jammed one inside the other, pour some cold water into the inner glass and stand the outer one in warm water. After a few moments they should easily separate. If you have the misfortune to break a glass, splinters and small bits can be picked up on wet cotton wool—which can be then thrown away—with no damage to your fingers.

## Cutlery

Not so long ago, the 'canteen of cutlery' was a traditional present from the bride or bridegroom's parents to the happy couple! Now cutlery is very often bought by place settings or sets as it can be afforded and a full set is built up over a period of time.

In recent years, stainless steel cutlery has become very popular with young people furnishing for the first time, or older people replacing worn-out cutlery. Not only are there some excellent designs to choose from, but stainless steel is very easy to care for and does not require the polishing and attention needed by solid silver or silver plate, nor is it so expensive.

What you choose will be, of course, a matter of personal taste, and if you decide to buy stainless steel you will have a choice of very modern designs or more traditional ones. A very popular pattern, **opposite**, is Alveston by Old Hall which would suit almost any design of china or glass, whether modern or not. When choosing cutlery, don't just go by the appearance but pick up the pieces and hold them as if you were eating. You will be surprised by the different 'balance' in different designs—and some of it may feel surprisingly clumsy in use.

To keep your cutlery in good condition, wash and dry it as soon as possible after use—particularly spoons and forks which may become stained by food being left on them. Make sure you dissolve powder detergents very well in the water, as some undissolved detergents can cause staining or pitting on cutlery. Salt, too, can have the same

effect under certain conditions, so guard against it by washing cutlery quickly and separately from plates and dishes. You can get egg stains off spoons and forks by rubbing them with salt, but make sure you wash them immediately in plain water, then in hot water and washing-up liquid.

Never put plastic or wooden knife handles in very hot water. Keep these dry as far as possible. Keep knives in a separate knife rack, not jumbled in a cutlery tray and, please, never be tempted to use a good table knife for odd jobs like tightening up a loose screw or cutting string!

Well-cared for, any well-designed and well made cutlery should give you many years of satisfactory service. Some makers of stainless steel cutlery now also make other beautiful pieces for the table, such as condiment sets, serving dishes, candlesticks. Look out for the ranges by Old Hall which blend well with their fine cutlery designs.

# II. *THE LOOK OF YOUR HOME*

We are not going to talk about colour in the terms that one is better than another, or more fashionable, because colour is such a personal matter. However, there are a few general rules which it is as well to know and understand, even if you then decide to throw them all out of the window and prove that, by following your own instinct, you can make the exceptions prove the rules.

*Illusions* Colours can be so illusory that by their clever use you can create an impression of constant sunshine where there is none; cool, clear water just outside the windows of a room that might well face a factory wall; a longer room; a squarer room, a higher or lower ceiling, whatever it is you feel your rooms are lacking.

You have to be very skilled in the use of colour to be able to create a harmonious scheme without the use of any neutral colours whatever. White, of course, is the obvious one, and you would be well advised to include some highlights in white paint, lamps and shades, china ornaments or cushions, somewhere in every room. Other neutral colours, like grey, cream and beige, used in the same way, also 'tone down' the stronger shades yet, by their very neutrality, give them emphasis.

Some colours—green, blue and grey, for instance—are generally thought of as being 'cool', and therefore more suitable for use in rooms where the windows face south. Such rooms can look and feel uncomfortably warm when the sun is streaming in, and the use of reds and oranges here could have the effect of flames dancing in the hearth.

Other colours—like reds and oranges—are considered 'warm', and suggested for use in rooms facing north, where it sometimes seems that the north wind doth blow, even in the middle of summer. Use yellow or orange, gold or red for curtains or window blinds in these rooms and give the impression that the sun never stops shining.

Never underestimate the power of colour. A quick look through a few magazines devoted to home furnishing and design will soon show you that it is the way a room is decorated, not by any means the amount spent on furnishing, that will impress you most. The humblest whitewood furniture, the simplest piece picked up at a jumble sale, the cheapest fabric run up into a clever drape, will hold admiring attention if—but only if—all the items are colour-keyed to a carefully worked out plan. No furniture, however fashionable or expensive, will look at its best, or repay you anything like its value, if it has been chosen willy-nilly, without any relation to the items around it.

So all this is good news! What we are saying is that a few cans of paint and rolls of wall-covering, in the right tones and shades, can do more for your home than the most expensive furniture in the world! Let's see how.

Start, if you can, by deciding which colours and effects, overall, please you most. Some people declare stoically that they just can't live with reds, and others, with equal firmness, profess that green always brings them bad luck. As we have said, it is not necessarily which colours you use, but how that matters.

Then think of your house, flat or maisonette in terms of a colour wheel, with the hall or landing as the pivot, and the rooms opening from it the colour lines leading from the centre. It is disconcerting to open door after door on to unrelated, strong colours and patterns, even though each one, in its own right, might be perfectly charming. Try to make the colour scheme of each room a development of the one before it. This kind of thinking, cleverly applied, does not show.

Suppose you chose a strikingly bold design of wall-covering for the hall, perhaps a swirling pattern in reds and blues on a white background. This could be the key to your other room schemes. In the kitchen, you could repeat one of the blue colours, perhaps a deep turquoise shade, toned down with white and grey, and with accents—in teatowels, poppy-patterned china, handles of utensils—of red. Notice the suggestion to use grey here: you would probably want to avoid too close an imitation of the national flag!

A north-facing room could reverse the colour scheming, concentrating on accentuating the reds in the hall wall-covering, again with some white, and with large areas of soft furnishings, such as curtains, a bedspread or sofa cover, in a pink, a paler shade of the red tone. Accents here could be in a sharp, clear blue.

In a bedroom, blues from the palest to deepest midnight could still owe their origin to the original wallpaper, but have a completely different personality.

Another way to unify a living area is to continue the same colour of floor-covering throughout the ground floor or first floor. If you are having floor tiles laid, you might consider having them in one colour, say avocado green, and then be as ingenious as you like, teaming this with a number of colours in the different rooms. Yellow, pink, strong blue, lavender, white—practically anything goes. If you are having fitted carpet, you could have the same colour, but in different qualities according to the needs of each room.

In any case, it is a mistake to change the floor-covering too often throughout an area. A much greater illusion of space is created by having, where practicable, a continuous colour. And, another advantage, there are less joins at doorways to ruck up or tear.

*Planned experiments*   As some of the heavier colours and patterns tend to be rather difficult to live with, it is wise to keep your greatest adventures in interior design for rooms which are used for only short periods at a time. Halls, for example, benefit from a bold design which will be exciting to see when one comes in through the door, and will create fresh interest when one passes from one room to another. Since the longest time you are likely to spend in the hall is when you are on the telephone, perhaps it is a good thing, from this point of view, too, to decorate it in such a way as to discourage lingering!

The dining room, unless it combines the living or sitting room, is an ideal candidate for an experiment in design. As you would rarely be there for more than a couple of hours at a time, you are not likely to tire of a 'busy' scheme. Do be sure, however, that the colours you choose complement the purpose of the room and would not be likely to put you off your food!

*A long narrow room*   Use colour to help you give your rooms the near-perfect proportions they might lack. If, for example, you have a room which appears too long and narrow—and especially if it is underfurnished at the moment—you can 'bring in' the two end walls by painting them a dark colour, or using a bold wallpaper and decorating the long walls in a paler shade, or white, grey or beige, or with a plain wallcovering. This is where the actual colour you use is not all-important, it is the way you use it that matters. You will achieve the diminishing effect equally well if you use dark blue teamed with a paler blue; dark green and grey-green, or deep pink and pastel pink— or any other similar combination you can think of. The same principle applies to a long, narrow hallway. A strong colour or bold pattern used on the end wall minimises the 'railway carriage' effect and causes the eye to skip over the intervening acres!

Red, particularly, has the effect of making surfaces seem closer to you than they really are, of bringing them together into the centre of the room, so avoid using it in quantity unless you want to create a cosy, intimate effect. A tiny square dining room, perhaps with a small circular table in the centre of the room, and subdued lighting, would look well painted or papered completely in red. But in a small living room, where one wanted to create a feeling of more leisure space and not of tripping over people's feet or the children's toys, an all-red scheme would be inappropriate.

*Lowering the ceiling*   If you have a room with a particularly high ceiling which, no matter how effective the heating, always appears cold and uninviting, you can visually lower the height by the use of a strong colour. Dark blue (and if blue is dark enough, it will NOT look cold) effectively stops the eye well short of the actual height of the room.

But if you have a serious height problem in a room, and you think it needs more than an illusionary coat of paint, you can usually put in a false ceiling below the original one. But before launching on a permanent feature such as this, do try fixing up a smallish panel in one corner, in the finish you plan to use, stand back and stare at it long and hard. Beware of overdoing it, and bringing the apparent—and actual—height of the ceiling down to the level of claustrophobia!

If yours is the opposite problem and you have a too-low ceiling, try the opposite colour tactic: paint it, for instance, a pastel colour—blue is good here—and, if possible, have two of the wall surfaces in the same colour, continuing right up and over the ceiling. If the room has a moulding just below the ceiling level—and many older houses have —paint over this, too, so that there is no break in the colour continuity. Any horizontal colour change reduces the apparent height of a wall.

*The use of patterns*   Patterns need care. Until one gains confidence in one's ability to mix and match, it is usually as well to apply the old maxim, 'Moderation in all things'. A room zinging with patterns of varying kinds can look fun and happy-go-lucky and right. But, more often than not, it will look like a haphazard collection of unrelated articles—which in fact it might be.

Generally, if you use one strong pattern for curtains, carpet, wallcovering or soft furnishing material, that is enough. For the rest of the room, you can use colours picked up from the pattern, and interesting textures. Hessian, heavy weaves, rush matting, 'sculptured' carpets, all have deep 'groovy' surfaces which cause the light to catch them at a number of different angles and almost create a pattern.

When you have assessed a room as it is, with one major pattern area, you can start adding other touches, such as patterned cushions on a plain chair or bedcover, patterned lampshades where they will be seen against a plain wall or curtain area, or a rug on a plain floorcovering. But do try to avoid setting one pattern directly on top of another.

All this talk about heavy and light colours, warm and cool ones, pattern or plain, but where, with the whole rainbow to choose from, do you begin? The inspiration for a colour scheme—if you are not already bubbling with ideas of your own—can come from a bed of flowers in the garden, a bluebell wood, a leafy lane on an autumn day,

the beach on a sunny seaside holiday . . . there are colour lessons to be learned all around us.

Whatever colours you choose, let the finished effect be a reflection of your personality, for the home you are building is uniquely yours and yours alone. Make sure that it complements and flatters your temperament, for you are the ones who will have to live with it!

---

*Imaginative use of patterned wallpaper adds a new dimension to the look of a room*

# Lighting

The whole aspect of any room at night can be transformed by the way you light it, and although it is very much a matter of personal taste, there are a few simple general hints to bear in mind when choosing your lighting.

First of all consider where lighting is needed for a specific purpose—over a dining table, for kitchen working, for reading in bed, on a desk; then where it can be used decoratively—for instance, a spotlight to pick out a picture, ornament or lamp that is a decoration in itself in a corner or on a shelf. With clever lighting, you can draw attention away from any bad features in a room for light automatically draws the eye, so make sure it shows up the things you want the eye to see!

As well as creating 'pools' of light for a specific purpose, background lighting will also be needed as the contrast between complete darkness and bright areas of light is uncomfortable to look at. This can be provided by diffused light such as a fluorescent tube placed behind a pelmet, a spotlight directed up at the ceiling or a lamp with an opaque shade which gives a soft, all-round light. It is a good idea to have light available from several sources in your main living room—in fact to have more than you will need at any one time, so that you can vary the emphasis at will and light your room for a party, for watching television, for reading and sewing, for having a meal, and so on.

It often happens, if moving into an old house, that you can be saddled with a ceiling fitting right in the middle of the room, or in a place which is quite out of keeping with your furniture arrangement. If so, you can hook a flex across the ceiling to where you want the light to hang and screw a small cup hook in the ceiling to hold it.

Lampshades and fittings tend to be expensive, but it is quite cheap and easy to make your own shades from frames bought from a craft shop or store and small quantities of material; we give you some hints on this in chapter 13. Don't despise the chain stores as a source of inexpensive light fittings. If you haven't already looked there, you may be surprised at the quality and good design of some of the fittings they have to offer.

*Spotlights*   A very versatile form of domestic lighting as they can be used for general lighting, to highlight a particular object or to provide diffused lighting. In a traditional type of room setting it would probably look better if the spotlight were concealed, whilst still performing its work, but spotlights are perfectly in keeping with modern decor. They can be placed in the corner of the room on standard lamp fittings or on industrial track run across the ceiling; the lamp fitting can be moved along the track to the exact position where it is required.

*Fluorescent tubes*   They give twice as much light as the ordinary bulb of the same wattage, keep much cooler and are therefore ideal for fitting behind pelmets, on bed-heads and under kitchen cabinets. They were originally thought of as giving a cold, hard light and were mainly used industrially or for shop lighting. However, it is now possible to buy a wide range of different tints, so make some enquiries before you decide on which one to choose. They will give very effective light, but should be used in conjunction with other lights if 'mood' is required!

*Kitchen needs*   The right kind and amount of lighting in a kitchen affects both efficiency and safety. There are four different needs here: overall lighting for the room; directional light which will illuminate specific working areas, such as the sink and the worktops where you will be preparing the food; the lighting which is built into equipment—diffused strips of light over the hobs of a cooker, and the lights which operate when you open the door of a refrigerator. And lastly, where necessary, lights inside cupboards.

The way you decorate your kitchen will have a bearing on the amount of light you will need to provide. Where the wall surfaces are, at one extreme, white tiles, and at the other, dark matt paint or wallcovering, the reflection and absorption qualities of the light will vary enormously. Glossy painted surfaces are not recommended, for although they reflect light and might apparently increase its effectiveness, in practice they produce a glare that is both unpleasant and uncomfortable to live and work with.

More than in any other room of the house, you will want to be sure that your light fittings in the kitchen can be kept scrupulously clean. For this reason, hanging flexes should be avoided and fittings chosen which are either recessed into the ceiling or placed close against it. These fittings have the added advantage of spreading the light across the ceiling area so that it is diffused downwards, rather than throwing an unwelcome shadow between you and your working surface.

Directional light over working areas can be in strip form, fitted to the fronts of the wall cupboards. Strips of light are available in tungsten or fluorescent forms, and both have the advantage of being shadow-free. Before installing fluorescent tubes, though, be sure that you are not one of the few people who are disturbed by the almost imperceptible flickering that this kind of light produces. The lights should be shaded from view, both when you are sitting and standing, by a continuous strip along the edge of the cupboard. Where there are no wall cupboards hung in convenient positions, directional lighting can be provided by ceiling spotlights beamed on to the area. Large cupboards, low ones or pantries can easily be fitted with lights which operate automatically when the door is opened and closed.

Finally, don't forget the garden. When you have time to get round to such refinements, lighting in the garden can make an attractive addition to your evening decor. Even one garden light fitting to highlight an attractive group of shrubs, a tree, pool or piece of statuary can look enormously impressive.

*Pools of light from individual lamps can give an air of cosiness and intimacy to the house at night*

# *12.* CLEANING THE PLACE

Coping with housework is really a matter of temperament. There's the attitude that cleanliness is next to godliness and no matter how tempting the weather outside or how tired one is feeling, every last little bit of the house must be tidy and sparkling. Or the other extreme, where so long as one has warmth and plenty to eat, the dust can collect and the house go untidied indefinitely. Neither of these attitudes really produces a home that is pleasant to live in or a wife it is a pleasure to live with—surely the objectives you and your husband are aiming for! It really pays, at the outset of your married life, or when making a change such as moving into a new house, to sit down and organise your (house) working life in a sensible and practical way so that you are master of the house, not the house master of you!

A positive attitude to the whole question of cleaning is something some people are born with—but it can be cultivated in the rest of us who are not so fortunate. A certain amount of planning and routine will give a framework which, once set up, can be a great help in dealing with day-to-day chores. In other words, plan it, do it, and forget about it. This is not to say that your framework should be completely inflexible—switch it round if it is going to fit in better with what you happen to be doing.

Your way of working and what you can do will, naturally, be quite different if you are still going out to work, and we will give some guidelines later in this chapter both for full-time housewives and for part-time ones. Whichever you are, you will still need good equipment, well organised, plenty of storage space so that the house or flat can be kept tidy, and a systematic way of working.

## Equipment

All equipment, whether large or small, should be carefully chosen so that it is of maximum use to you—and sometimes a small item such as a kitchen plate rack or the right sort of hand brush or mop for a particular job can save you hours of work.

The organisation of your broom cupboard we have already dealt with, and keeping this part of the kitchen always in workmanlike order is very good for morale. Polishes, dusters etc. can travel round the house with you more easily if you keep them in a portable rack or basket.

If you have room for it, a basket-on-wheels would be ideal and save you a lot of to-and-froing to fetch forgotten items. In it you can keep furniture polish, metal polish, window polish, liquid cleaner for windows and tiles, dustpan and brush, several dusters and a wet-use cloth. If you have no room in the bathroom for special lavatory and other cleaners and disinfectant, make a corner for these, too.

Set aside a short time each week for such jobs as emptying the vacuum cleaner (there's no nastier a job than dealing with a cleaner packed solid with dust), removing hairs from carpet sweeper, checking that equipment is in good order and washing dusters and brushes. It is a good idea to pin up a list of polishes etc. in your broom cupboard and mark on this when anything needs renewing.

An essential in any kitchen today is a holder and roll of paper kitchen towels—for quick mopping up. In fact, a roll can be included in the basket of cleaning materials to great advantage.

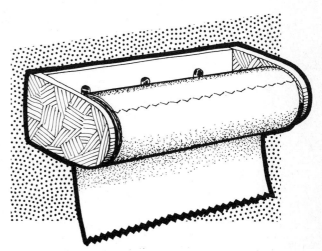

## For the Working Wife

Obviously, if you are out at work, any short cuts you can take will be all to the good, particularly if you find yourself coping with a new house, new husband and your usual job all at the same time. Many working wives say that the first year of married life left them completely exhausted for naturally, on top of everything else, they wanted to do a good deal of entertaining and there were a number of decorating and do-it-yourself jobs on hand, too.

If you are in this situation, keep your daily work in the house as simple as possible. If you can get up in time to make the bed, do the breakfast washing up and give the bathroom a wipe round before going to work, so much the better. You do have one advantage over a full-time house-wife at home with children—when you come home in the evening things will be as you left them and not more untidy!

In the evening having, we hope, been given a hand with the supper washing up, find ten minutes before going to bed to tidy the living room, empty ashtrays, throw away newspapers, plump up cushions and stack up magazines.

This simple routine will keep your house or flat looking fairly respectable in general, and if you can set aside a couple of evenings or a weekend morning each week for more thorough cleaning you shouldn't find life too hard. Obviously the living room, kitchen and bathroom will need attention once a week, but bedroom, windows, etc. will probably get by with less frequent thorough cleaning.

Another saving in time is to organise bulk supermarket shopping and washing at the launderette (if you haven't a washing machine) at the same time so that both loads can be brought back together by car (if you have no car, and the distance isn't too far, it can pay to take a taxi). This might not need doing more than once a fortnight, perishable foods being bought in lunch hours as needed. The washing load can be dealt with at the launderette whilst you are doing the supermarket shopping, to save time, and you can often fit this in after work if both launderette and supermarket stay open late in the evenings.

If you have storage space, another saver, both in money and time, is to buy in bulk. Things like soap, detergents, proprietary cleaners, lavatory paper and so on are always going to be needed and not only do you get cheaper rates by buying in large quantities and save on shopping time, but you win when prices go up and you have bought at a lower rate. With less storage space, you could arrange with a friend to share bulk buys, thus giving you both an advantage.

Another time-saver is to put away your linen table-cloths and napkins for some future, more leisurely phase, when you can spend time washing and ironing, and invest in paper ones—not so pleasant to use, but your food will not taste any worse and you will have more leisure to enjoy it.

Cut down on oven-cleaning (if you're not the proud possessor of one of those super new ovens that are self-cleaning) by using self-basting roasting tins, line dishes and grill pan whenever you can with household foil—and

wherever possible prevent splashes and stains inside the cooker. If you do get splashes, wipe them off whilst the oven is still warm (not hot). This will save much scraping and work later when the fat etc. has had time to become thoroughly burned on.

An efficient plate rack on which you can leave every-day dishes and cups to drain is also a great help. If buying a new refrigerator, one which automatically de-frosts itself will save you another chore.

Persuade the bathroom to be self-cleaning as far as possible. Always use some form of water-softener such as bath salts, bubble bath and so on and encourage your husband to do the same (or use washing soda if he finds bath salts too effeminate!). In this way you will avoid having to scrub off a thick grease ring from the bath every day. Make sure your lavatory has a block cleaner hanging in it, or the type which you fit inside the cistern which dispenses a cleaner/disinfectant liquid into the lavatory at each flush. This can save a lot of sprinkling with powders and brushing with brushes.

Finally, set aside a large drawer or small cupboard as a 'junk hole', where you can throw things which you want to keep but have no time to deal with as you are tidying round. Newspapers and magazines from which you want to take clippings, washing instruction labels from clothes (write on which garment each applies to), operating instructions for household equipment, oddments of all kinds can go in there for periodical sorting and filing. In the office, it would be a 'Miscellaneous' file, and you know how indispensable that can be!

## For the Full-time Housewife

If you are in the position of being able to give more time to your housework, perhaps because you are home with babies or small children to look after, too, don't despise any of the foregoing hints you may find useful. There is really no virtue in doing things the long way round if a short-cut will serve equally well, and there cannot be many women who could not use a little extra free time.

If there are people in the house all the time, you will find the disadvantage that it gets dirtier and untidier than if you were all out at work. It is particularly difficult to keep an open-plan house, with kitchen leading off from a combined living/dining room, looking at its best, especially when there are children (and their friends) about. In this situation, storage space—plenty of it—and a place for everything are really the basic essentials. Half the battle in quick and effective cleaning is having as little clutter to contend with as possible. The other half of the battle, which many women have to fight, is the battle against boredom—yet another reason for getting through routine jobs as quickly and efficiently as possible. One housewife we know gears her housework to her moods. When in a rage with life in general or someone in particular she tackles an energetic job, such as window cleaning, which she claims gets done in half the usual time. If feeling lethargic, she turns on the washing machine and does a few loads of laundry, whilst catching up on the (saved) Sunday papers and magazines. This is all very well if the theory is not carried too far. A placid person might find her windows never got cleaned, while her clothes were always in the wash.

Here is a suggested working routine—subject, of course, to individual variation.

*Daily work*  Go quickly round each room, tidying up and doing minimal cleaning to make it habitable. A portable radio carried round with you speeds the work along!

Many people like to start by dealing with the kitchen, but others advocate beginning upstairs and working down, ending up with the kitchen. As this method can save going up and down through rooms that have already been cleaned, we will suggest a routine based on this.

*Bedrooms*  When you get up, open windows, turn back bedclothes, tidy up and remove any glasses, cups or used ashtrays to the kitchen when you go down to get the breakfast. Come upstairs after breakfast bringing cleaning materials, vacuum or carpet sweeper and mop. Make beds, empty all wastepaper baskets into one. Finish tidying, dust furniture and ledges. Go through rooms with vacuum cleaner or sweeper and mop surrounds if necessary. Straighten furniture and curtains, close windows. Leave debris on landing to be thrown away.

*Bathroom*  Open window and tidy up talcum powder, etc. into bathroom cabinet. Arrange towels neatly. Wash toothglasses and wipe over shelves. Wash handbasin, ledges and bath (use disinfectant in the water, if you like). Wipe lavatory seat, cistern handle etc. and brush out lavatory if necessary. Clean floor and close window.

*Landing*  Dust any ledges and go over carpet with vacuum or carpet sweeper. Take downstairs any rubbish to be disposed of, then sweep or vacuum down the stairs.

*Living/dining room(s)*  Open windows, tidy up, remove breakfast dishes. Pile up objects that don't belong there for re-distribution to other rooms. Empty ashtrays, throw out old newspapers, throw away dead flowers, sort post into letters and bills and file (put bills on a bulldog clip hanging in a convenient place for husband or you to deal with periodically!). If you have a fire or stove, clean out ashes and wipe hearth. Dust furniture and remove any sticky spots with a wet cloth. Vacuum carpet and surrounds. Set furniture to rights and generally make the room look neat. Close windows.

*Hall*  Try to clean thoroughly each day with vacuum cleaner, or if a hard floor, with broom and mop, as trodden-in grit can quickly ruin the floor or carpet. Shake out doormat, dust hall table or ledges.

*Kitchen*  Wash up dishes, ashtrays, flower vases, etc. Wipe over cooker and any surfaces that have been splashed. Empty waste bucket, wastepaper baskets and any accumulated rubbish. Clean kitchen floor and sink. Re-distribute ashtrays, etc. to their rightful places.

You are now ready (after a cup of coffee and a few minutes' relaxation) to do some shopping, washing or ironing, window-cleaning, baking or one of the more thorough cleaning jobs in one selected room, some brief suggestions for which we now make.

*Living/dining room(s)*  Collect together all small ornaments, clocks, pictures, coffee table, etc., take them out of the room, and open the windows.

Remove the dust from high up in the room (*i.e.* on picture rails, pelmet tops, ceiling corners, lampshades, etc.) with the correct vacuum attachment or with a feather duster. Continue down the walls with the cleaner attachment or with a broom covered with a clean duster.

Go over curtains with a stiff brush or cleaner attachment, and put net curtains to soak whilst you do the other work.

Go over tops of books with vacuum cleaner attachment or small soft brush.

Dust all wood surfaces, removing any marks, and wipe over paintwork with water and a proprietary cleaning preparation. Polish furniture with a good wax polish and rub over window ledges and other painted surfaces.

Clean the insides of the windows.

Vacuum upholstered furniture, getting well down the sides and backs of chair seats where debris collects. Feel down first to remove any hard objects—perhaps that 50p piece your husband lost last week. Next deal with carpet surrounds, turning them back to clean unless they are tacked down. Use crevice vacuum attachment in this case.

Go over carpet and surrounds and polish fireplace.

Replace furniture.

Rinse and hang out net curtains. Wash or polish small ornaments. Replace when dry and clean.

*Kitchen*  Turn out one or two cupboards every time you give the kitchen a thorough clean, and wash the cupboard when empty, re-lining if necessary.

De-frost the refrigerator every week or fortnight.

Wash walls with water and a proprietary cleaner and clean inside windows. Wash all paint and working surfaces (you can use the type of cleaner which does not need rinsing off afterwards, to save work).

Wipe down equipment and plate rack and see if cooker needs any more cleaning attention. Now is the time to polish any enamelled equipment with a silicone cream to give it protection against corrosion.

Clean the floor carefully, removing marks with fine steel wool, if appropriate, and polish with a non-slip polish, if necessary. Thoroughly clean the sink (though you will, of course, do this every day or two as well).

*Bedrooms*  Again take one or two drawers and cupboards at a time and tidy them out. Remove small ornaments to be replaced later.

Proceed as for living room, cleaning walls, paintwork, and windows and putting net curtains to soak.

Strip the bed and brush the mattress, turning it from top to bottom, or side to side if it is a spring interior mattress. Shake all blankets thoroughly in the open air. Make up the bed, turning the sheets to equalise the wear (*i.e.* sometimes put the broad hem at the top of the bed, and sometimes at the bottom).

Clean the carpet and surrounds, as for living room.

Dust and polish furniture and replace. Wash ornaments and return to their place. Hang nets when clean and dry.

*Bathroom*  Clean thoroughly as for daily routine, but wipe over walls, light fittings and windows. Also polish handles, metal fittings, bath racks etc. Wash curtains from time to time.

*Landing and hall*  Dust and wash paintwork on front door and porch, clean glass, polish door handles. Sort out coat cupboard or under-stairs 'glory hole'. Dust walls.

Dust and polish furniture, window ledges and bannisters.

Clean carpets very thoroughly, removing stair rods one at a time. Say twice a year, change position of stair carpet to even wear.

Polish all hard surfaces and clean and polish any mirrors.

## Spring Cleaning

We don't propose to give you hints on spring cleaning—basically it is thorough cleaning only more so! If you turn up your carpet edges once a fortnight to vacuum underneath, you take up the whole carpet and underlay and vacuum back and front. If you brush dust off the light fittings from time to time, take them down completely and wash or clean according to type. And so on. All cupboards should be completely tidied out so that they are empty enough to accumulate the forthcoming year's contents.

## Better Organization

Suppose, however hard you try, your house still seems to be in a continual mess—a clean mess, but still a mess! This seems to be the bane of some of us who work as hard as others, but who just haven't the knack of making things look tidy.

If this is your problem, you just have to take yourself—or rather your home—in hand. Remember the saying about the Frenchwoman who achieves her slick and well-groomed appearance because, after dressing and making ready for a party, she looks in the mirror and removes all the pieces of jewellery she is wearing but one!

Take the same sort of look at your living room. Go in there one morning and remove every piece of bric-a-brac, magazine or picture in sight. Now choose one or two of the simplest ornaments, vases or ashtrays and replace them, storing the rest away to take their turn later. Buy or make a rack for magazines, or save a special corner for them, throwing out or giving away any that become out of date. Make it a rule never to have more than half-a-dozen at a time.

Keep letters to be answered, papers, bills in box files and put these on the bookshelves if you have no desk.

Always, if you have a fire or stove, or gas appliance, keep the hearth neat, clean and sparkling. The eye is always drawn there as it tends to be the focal point in the room.

Take the same critical look at other rooms in the house and put away everything that is needed but not immediately wanted to hand. If you are short of storage space, organise more. For instance, buy lockers to go under beds—they hold a great deal—or if they are too costly, large cardboard boxes are a good substitute. If you are buying a new coffee table, look at the type which is really a box with a lifting lid. Tidying children's books or games into it at the end of the day takes one minute. An old tin trunk bought cheaply at a jumble sale and painted with a bright polyurethane paint can serve in the hall as a container for children's wellington boots or shoes—and save yet more mud being tracked into the house.

Set aside a cupboard for 'dead storage'—that is, things which will be seldom used but might come in useful some day. It is no good having these items mixed up with things in current use. The same goes for winter and summer clothes. They should be sorted out, cleaned and packed in polythene bags until they are wanted for the next season.

If you get easily disorganised, make lists to help you. A pad with tear-off sheets fixed inside a kitchen cupboard door with a pencil firmly attached to it by a piece of string is an invaluable aide-memoire.

Basic tidiness makes cleaning easier, which gives you more time for being basically tidier, which gives you that most precious of all commodities—leisure to enjoy life!

# Stain Removal

Before leaving the subject of cleaning, it might be helpful to give some general advice on removing stains, both from household furnishings and clothes. It pays to have a box to hand containing the various products which will help you to get out stains quickly and easily, together with a stock of clean rags with which to work.

These are the products which will be useful to you in stain removal, but do remember to label all the bottles and containers clearly and keep them well out of the reach of children.

| | |
|---|---|
| Ammonia | Helps to neutralise acid stains, but must be used with care as it can affect some dyes. Dilute with at least three parts of water and use in a room with the window open. |
| Borax | Useful for removing tea stains. |
| Carbon tetrachloride | Useful for removing most greasy marks. Should be used with care (as should proprietary products based on carbon tetrachloride) as the fumes can be dangerous if inhaled. Work with the window open and make sure the bottle is left well corked up, pouring a little at a time into a dish as you need it. Do not smoke when using it and do not iron over an article which has just been spot-cleaned with it until the fumes have completely evaporated. Work on the wrong side of the fabric holding an absorbent pad of clean cotton on the right side and gently rubbing with a cloth on the wrong side. Always work from the outside to the centre of a stain. |
| Cornflour or French chalk | Keep a supply handy for absorbing stains. |
| Glycerine | Useful generally as a solvent for stains such as fruit juice or coffee and is particularly good if the stain is old and set in hard. Articles should be rinsed well after application of glycerine. |
| Hydrogen peroxide | A good bleach to use on white articles but should be well diluted (about one part hydrogen peroxide to nine parts water is usual). |
| Methylated spirit | For removing stains such as ball-point pen. |
| Vinegar | Useful for some stains such as beer or perspiration, and a standard part of the larder anyway. Use well diluted—2 tablespoons to a pint of water. |

There are, of course, many proprietary products which can be used, and even complete stain removal kits ready assembled for you. However you will probably find it cheaper to keep the components above.

First essential in dealing with stains is speed—your speed. Out with the stain remover and deal with the disaster immediately. Sometimes, if the stain is on washable fabric, immediate soaking in cold water followed by washing in the usual way will take it out without any more drastic action.

Old stains which are set into fabric are much more difficult to deal with—besides, you may even have forgotten what it was that caused them. So do act quickly if at all possible.

There are different types of stains. Stains by liquids are absorbed by the fibres; stains caused by such substances as paint or tar which are absorbed very little or not at all; and stains such as blood which have the characteristics of both categories.

If you don't know what the stain is and it has been set for some time into the fabric, it is really better, after a few cautious experiments, to seek professional advice and take it to a reputable dry-cleaner, who should have the skill to identify and treat it for you.

Before treating any stain, particularly on delicate fabric, or fabric which is not colourfast, test the inside of a seam or hem with the chemical or substance you are going to use to make sure that there won't be any fading or shrinking.

The following list of some common stains and how to remove them should help you when that moment of crisis arrives!

| Stain | Washable Fabric | Non-washable Fabric |
| --- | --- | --- |
| Ballpoint pen | Dab with cotton-wool or rag dipped in methylated spirit, renewing rag when soiled. Wash at once in warm suds. | Apply methylated spirit, wipe off with clean cloth. |
| Beer | Wash at once in normal way. If still stained, add vinegar to water, wash and rinse. | Sponge with clear water and dab dry. If unsuccessful, sponge with vinegar and water, then rinse with clear water. |
| Blood | Soak in cold salt water or hydrogen peroxide (dilute) then wash as usual. If stains are still there soak for a longer period. Rinse well. | Brush well. Sponge with clear water or water with a little added ammonia. Rinse well and dab dry. |
| Chewing gum | Rub with an ice cube, then pick or scrape off with a spoon. If stained, sponge with carbon tetrachloride. Wash. | As for washable fabrics, but omit washing. |
| Chocolate or cocoa | Scrape off as much as possible, then soak in borax solution (1 ounce to 1 pint water). Rinse and wash. If stubborn, sprinkle with borax whilst damp, leave for half-an-hour, then wash. | Scrape off and sponge with cloth wrung out in borax solution or use carbon tetrachloride. |
| Cod-liver oil | Wash in hot, soapy water and rinse well. If stubborn, take immediately to dry-cleaners. | Treat with carbon tetrachloride or take to dry-cleaners. |
| Coffee | For fresh stains on linen or cotton, rinse well in boiling water, then wash. For other fabrics, use hot water. If stains have dried, add glycerine to the water, sprinkle with borax, then pour water through, and wash. | Apply glycerine, leave for a few hours, then sponge with water. |
| Cream | Soak in warm water, then launder. | Sponge with carbon tetrachloride, allow to dry, then sponge with warm water. |
| Egg | Scrape off as much as possible, rub with cold salt water and wash. If stain remains, use carbon tetrachloride. | Scrape off, sponge with cold water, then with warm suds. Allow to dry, and if necessary, use carbon tetrachloride. |
| Fruit and fruit juice | Sponge with cold water with a little added glycerine and leave for an hour. Sponge with white vinegar, then launder. | Apply glycerine and leave for an hour. Rub with carbon tetrachloride. |
| Grass | Soak in methylated spirits, then rinse in warm water. | Sponge with methylated spirit and leave to dry. |
| Gravy | Wash in cool suds. If stain remains, use carbon tetrachloride. | Use carbon tetrachloride. Sponge with warm water. |
| Grease and oil | Use carbon tetrachloride, then launder. For buttery stains cover with a borax paste, leave for an hour, launder. | For all greasy marks, apply a paste made from French chalk and carbon tetrachloride. Allow to dry, then brush off. Another method: fold clean blotting paper around stain and press with hot iron. |

| Stain | Treatment | Alternative |
|---|---|---|
| Ice cream | Wipe off, then soak in cool suds, wash in hot water and rinse. Remove any remaining stains with carbon tetrachloride. | Sponge with borax solution, wipe with damp cloth and rub dry. If stain remains, use carbon tetrachloride. |

| Stain | Treatment | Alternative |
|---|---|---|
| Ink | If you are quick, rinsing and washing in warm suds will get the stain out. If stubborn, sprinkle white fabric with salt and rub with cut lemon. Leave for an hour, rinse and wash. Soak coloured material in lukewarm milk, then wash. | Sponge with warm water. Take to dry-cleaners if stain won't come out. |
| Jam | If normal washing won't remove the marks, soak in warm borax solution, then wash. | Sponge with warm suds. If stain remains, rub with dry borax, leave, then dab off with a damp cloth. |
| Lipstick | Rub in glycerine, then launder in usual way, using hot water as the fabric allows. If stain persists, use carbon tetrachloride. | Rub in glycerine, dab on a little diluted ammonia, then sponge with a damp cloth. If stain persists, try carbon tetrachloride. |
| Milk | Rinse in cold water, wash as usual. If still stained, sprinkle with borax and soap flakes or detergent, pour on hot water and rub gently. Leave, then rinse and launder. | Apply carbon tetrachloride, leave to dry. Sponge with lukewarm water. |
| Nail varnish | Scrape off as much as possible, then treat immediately with nail varnish remover (except rayon- and acetate-containing fabrics which would be damaged by it. These need professional dry-cleaning.) Use methylated spirit if a mark remains. | Same as for washable fabrics. |
| Perspiration | Sponge with weak vinegar or ammonia solution, then wash. Rinse and wash in usual way if stain is fresh. | Sponge with methylated spirit then dab dry. |
| Scorch marks | If fibres are undamaged, cover with paste of borax and glycerine, leave for a few hours, then wash. If marks are very light, soaking in milk may work. Rinse well. | Sponge with borax solution (1 teaspoon borax to $\frac{1}{2}$ pint hot water), then with clear water. |
| Sea water | Brush out loose salt, soak in warm water, then launder. | Sponge with warm water to remove salt. |
| Soot | Shake off loose soot (do not rub or you will rub more in), wash in hot soapy water. | Sponge with carbon tetrachloride. |

| Stain | Washable Fabric | Non-washable Fabric |
|-------|-----------------|---------------------|
| Tar | Scrape off excess, then sponge with carbon tetrachloride. Rinse in warm water, then launder. | As for washable fabric, except for laundering. |
| Tea | Soak fresh stain in cold water then soak in hot borax solution. Leave until cold, then rinse and wash. For set stains, make a borax and water paste, work into stain then pour on hot water. Rinse and wash. | Rub glycerine into the stain and leave for a few hours. Dab with carbon tetrachloride. |
| Urine | Rinse in cold water, then launder. If stain remains, rinse thoroughly, then rinse again in vinegar solution. | Sponge immediately with cold water. If still stained, rinse in diluted ammonia, then vinegar solution. |
| Wine | Pour salt on as soon as spilt. Soak in hot borax solution, leave until cold, then rinse and wash. | Sponge in warm borax solution, rub dry. Repeat treatment until stain disappears. |

## Floor Care—Carpets

* During the first few weeks, a new carpet may tend to fluff and shed a little pile. This is normal. Do not clean too vigorously, and do not shampoo the carpet, but give it time to 'settle down'. If a few single tufts of pile stand up, trim them off with scissors. It is advisable to use your carpet sweeper only at first (for a month or so), then vacuum once or twice a week. Always brush or clean in the natural direction of the pile.
* To lengthen carpet's life, avoid wearing crepe and rubber-soled shoes and metal-tipped heels in the house. Lift furniture to move it, rather than dragging it across the carpet. Rearrange carpet, or alternatively the room, from time to time to even out wear. Or place rugs or mats in areas of heavy wear.

* Occasionally shampoo your carpet, following manufacturer's instructions carefully and allowing the carpet to dry thoroughly before replacing furniture. Or have carpet professionally cleaned.
* Deal with stains promptly, removing spilled liquid with paper tissues or a clean cloth and greasy spills with a knife or spoon. When cleaning with a proprietary solvent (read instructions carefully) or substance such as one table-spoon of ammonia in a cup of water, rub gently, starting at outer edge of stain and working towards centre. Change area of cloth used frequently and blot well between each application of cleaning fluid. Use solvents with great care on carpets with rubber or plastic backings as they could cause damage. Otherwise use a synthetic neutral liquid detergent (the kind which contains no bleach, such as used for washing delicate fabrics), in lukewarm water and apply lather with an absorbent cloth and blot off. Repeat until stain has gone, then repeat with clear water. Do not wet carpet too much, and allow to dry thoroughly before replacing furniture. In fact, it is a good idea to place a half-inch of clean white absorbent material (*i.e.* a wad of tissues) over the damp area and weight it down, leaving it for six or seven hours, to get rid of as much moisture as possible.

  If you have any doubts about which formula to use, test a little on an inconspicuous part of the carpet to see if dye has bled or it has affected the carpet in any way. If in doubt, have the carpet professionally cleaned.
* If you have a sisal carpet, care is very similar to above, but shampoo as little as possible. Vacuum regularly and spot-clean stains. When you do shampoo, keep carpet as dry as possible. Using a sponge and lather work gently over half a square yard at a time, mopping up dirt and foam without scrubbing vigorously. Overlap previously cleaned patch to avoid tide marks. Rinse lightly (do not saturate). The carpet must be secured at edges to prevent possible shrinkage. Do not walk on the carpet while it is still damp.

## Floor Care—Hard Surface

* If you are laying, or having laid, new hard flooring, enquire at the time you buy it the best type of polish or treatment to use to keep it looking good. This will save you trouble in the long run, and if you left a note about it pinned up inside the broom cupboard door when you moved on to your next house, you would earn the grateful thanks of the new owners! A Minit mop with an assortment of click-on heads will give you invaluable aid in all floor-cleaning jobs.
* There are two main types of polish—solvent-based wax polish and water-based wax polishes (water-based

emulsions). The first type includes the normal paste wax and liquid wax, and the second the self-shining type and the type which can be buffed up by a polishing machine. It is important to use the right type of polish for your floor as some types of flooring can be harmed by the wrong polish.

★ The following brief list will give you a guide to which type of polish to use on which floor. However, you must make sure that you know the composition of your floor, and also read instructions on the tin when buying the polish to check detailed use.

*Linoleum*  Use water-based emulsion polish on sealed linoleum; paste or liquid wax on unsealed linoleum.

*Cork*  On treated surfaces use either a solvent-based wax or water-based emulsion. If the surface is sealed, ask professional advice on maintaining it.

*Rubber flooring*  Use only water-based emulsion polish, and that occasionally. Wipe over with clear water in between. Avoid polish build-up by occasionally rubbing over with steel wool dipped in detergent solution. Rinse thoroughly and dry immediately before re-polishing.

*Thermoplastic tiles*  Polish with water-based emulsion polish.

*Vinyl flooring*  Very little polishing is needed usually, but if you want to do it occasionally, use water-based emulsion polish.

*Quarry tiles*  On old tiles, use coloured tile polish to match the tile and hide cracks or marks. On new, sealed tiles, use self-shining emulsion polish.

*Wood floors*  If sealed, use either type of polish, with a slight preference for solvent-based wax, particularly if the seal is no longer very new.

## Care of Upholstered Furniture

Light surface dirt on upholstery fabrics such as velveteen, tapestry, moquette, etc. can generally be removed by wiping over with a cloth dampened with carbon tetra-chloride, after you have swept off or vacuumed with the upholstery tool to remove loose fluff and dust.

If the upholstery is very dirty, the time has come to shampoo it, having first tested for colour-fastness in some inconspicuous place. Use a special upholstery cleaner and whisk up to a foam, and dampen a cloth or brush with it to rub lightly over the upholstery. Wipe over with a damp cloth and dry with a clean dry one. Work on one small area at a time, overlapping each one so that there won't be hard lines between the treated sections.

If you buy a new suite in a delicate-coloured fabric, it might be worth having it treated at the outset to make it dirt- and stain-repellent with some preparation such as Scotchgard. Enquire at the shop where you buy your suite.

## Care of Wooden Furniture

If you clean wooden furniture regularly with a good furniture polish, there should be few problems in keeping it in good condition. However, occasionally bloom forms through the room being damp. If polish is applied on a damp surface, moisture is trapped underneath and bloom forms. To treat this, mix a tablespoon of vinegar in a pint of warm water, wring out a soft rag in this and rub hard over the affected surface. Dry with a warm cloth and rub thoroughly. Let the furniture dry completely and then re-polish, using silicone cream on a wax-polished surface and liquid silicone on cellulose lacquered or French polished surfaces.

## Coping with Washday

Although there are so many mechanical aids to help with the laundry these days, there are also many more fabrics with special finishes, synthetics and mixtures of fibres to confuse the housewife. Many garments now carry a label giving advice on washing and ironing, but not all do, so the following table will prove helpful:

| | Machine wash | Hand wash |
|---|---|---|
| White cotton and linen articles without special finishes | Very hot maximum wash (85°C) to boil | Hand-hot (48°C) or boil |
| | *Spin or wring dry* | |
| Cottons, linens or rayons without special finishes, where colours are fast at 60°C | Hot maximum wash (60°C) | Hand-hot (48°C) |
| | *Spin or wring dry* | |
| Cottons, linens or rayons where colours are fast at 40°C but not at 60°C | Warm medium wash (40°C) | Warm (40°C) |
| | *Spin or wring dry* | |
| White nylon (do not wash with any other fabrics) | Hot medium wash (60°C) | Hand-hot (48°C) |
| | *Cold rinse, short spin or drip-dry* | |
| Coloured nylon; Terylene; cottons and rayon with special finishes; acrylic/cotton mixtures | Hand-hot medium wash (48°C) | Hand-hot (48°C) |
| | *Cold rinse, short spin or drip-dry* | |
| Wool, including close woven blankets, and wool mixtures with cotton or rayon | Warm minimum wash (40°C) | Warm wash (40°C) (Do not rub) |
| | *Spin (do not hand wring)* | |

| | Machine wash | Hand wash |
|---|---|---|
| Acrilan, Courtelle and Orlon; acetate and Tricel, including mixtures with wool; Terylene/wool blends | Warm minimum wash (40°C) *Cold rinse, short spin (do not wring)* | Warm (40°C) |
| Washable pleated garments containing Acrilan, Courtelle, Orlon, nylon, Terylene or Tricel | Do not machine wash *Drip-dry* | Warm (40°C) Warm rinse. Hand-hot final rinse. |
| Glass fibre | Do not machine wash *Drip-dry (do not iron)* | Warm water. |

## Ironing Temperature

Most modern dry irons have delicate temperature controls, generally with four numbered settings, sometimes with five: steam irons, which are either of the drip or spray variety, have only one temperature setting.

Very briefly, the following fabrics require the temperature settings indicated:

Setting 1 (Cool): synthetic fabrics such as Acrilan and Orlon.

Setting 2 (Warm): nylon, wool, triacetate, acetate, silk.

Setting 3 (Medium): rayon, easy-care cottons and linens.

Setting 4 (Hot): cotton, linen.

Setting 5 (Very Hot): seldom needed, but may be used sometimes for very heavy linen.

# 13. SEW IT YOURSELF

If you can spare some time and have a sewing machine (or access to one), you will be able to save a considerable amount of money by sewing such things as curtains, cushion covers, lampshades and loose covers yourself. When you look round the shops and see that huge, chunky floor cushions can cost up to £16 each, it can be rather discouraging, until you discover that the uncovered pads cost only £3 to £4 and realise that you can make the cover from less than 3 yards of 48-inch furnishing fabric! Lined curtains with fancy headings will cost you a good deal if made up by a shop (although you may find some shops which will make up simple unlined curtains free if you buy your fabric there). But with the variety of easy-to-use tapes available now, it is not an impossible job to tackle yourself. The following general hints will help you.

## Making Curtains

The first thing to decide is what type of curtain you need for your particular room. This will depend on its size, lightness, proportions of the window and the effect you want to achieve. There are three generally accepted standard curtain lengths, to just above the sill, a few inches below and to just above floor level.

On the whole, unless you have a special type of house such as a country cottage, floor-length curtains look best in living and dining rooms. In bedrooms, curtains often hang just below sill level, although you could have floor-length curtains here as well. Bathroom and kitchen curtains generally hang about an inch above the sill.

*Measuring up* To estimate the quantity of fabric you will need, measure the windows and allow 4 inches extra on finished length required for light curtains and 7 inches extra for heavier fabrics. Allow also an amount for the heading—usually double the finished heading depth. If the heading is particularly elaborate or unusual, allow extra if necessary.

You will also need to estimate the number of fabric widths and this will depend partly on the type of heading you choose—pinch pleats, for example, requiring a greater fabric allowance than a simple gathered heading. However, as a general guideline, you will require at least $1\frac{1}{2}$

times and up to 3 times the width of the curtain track for heavy- and medium-weight fabrics, and at least twice the width of the track for nets and sheers.

Multiply the curtain track accordingly and add on allowances for side hems and joinings. This measurement, divided by the width of your chosen curtain fabric, will give you the number of widths you will need and if you multiply by the length (including allowances) you will find the total number of yards required. Remember that if you choose a large pattern you must allow extra fabric for matching up. The salesman in the shop will be able to tell you the size of the pattern repeat and help you work out the allowance needed. It always looks better if a complete pattern runs across the top of the curtain. It is also a good idea to allow an extra inch or two in the yard as a shrinkage allowance, unless you are sure the fabric is shrink-proof. Always be generous in your width allowance. Nothing looks worse than skimpy curtains.

For example, for a curtain to hang on a track 6 feet wide, with a drop of 8 feet finished length, you would need the following amount of plain, medium heavy fabric, 48 inches wide:

| | |
|---|---|
| To find the number of widths, multiply track width by $2\frac{1}{2}$ | = 15 feet |
| To nearest multiple of 48 inches | = 16 feet |
| Therefore number of widths | = 4 widths giving side, hem and joining allowance |
| Four drops of 8 feet | = 32 feet |
| *Plus* | |
| Four times 7 inches hem allowance | = 2 feet 4 inches |
| Four times 3 inches heading allowance | = 1 foot |
| Shrinkage allowance | = 1 foot |
| As there would be no pattern-matching allowance, total | = 36 feet 4 inches |

Cutting the hem allowance down to 6 inches instead of 7 inches, you would need 12 yards of fabric for your curtain.

*Linings* Generally speaking, it is good policy to line curtains, as linings help to keep curtains clean, protect them from fading and make them drape better. (This does not apply of course to nets and sheers, and fabrics with the design showing on both sides.) You can put in a permanent lining in which case it is washed with the curtain. Alternatively you can make a detachable lining, using a special curtain tape which allows the lining to be fixed by the ordinary hanging hooks. There are obvious advantages in making a detachable lining, as it can be taken off for more frequent washing; if curtain and lining are washed separately there is far less bulk to put in the washing machine, to handle and to iron, and the same lining can be used, if necessary, for summer and winter curtains.

*To make a curtain with a fixed lining* First cut the curtain out, making quite sure that it is cut on the straight of the fabric. Pin the widths together, tack and machine, then press open the seams, snipping into any selvedges to prevent puckering.

Next cut out and join lining widths to match the curtain, making them about 3 inches shorter. Spread the curtain flat on the floor, wrong side up, then lay the lining over it, right side up, with both top edges level. If you want to make the curtain in a very thorough and professional way, you can fix the lining into the curtain at this stage by rows of long, loose 'locking' stitches—two rows down each 48-inch width. These prevent the lining hanging away from the curtain when it is hung up. For a single width, turn back a third of the lining from one side and take long, loose blanket stitches right down the lining, 3-4 inches apart, to fix it to the main curtain fabric. Stop a few inches short of the lower edge. Turn back a third of the lining from the other edge, and work in the same way (*see* below).

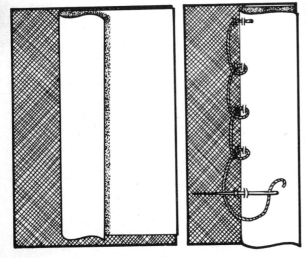

To finish the curtain, whether the lining is locked in or not, take turnings of about 1½ inches along each side edge of the curtain fabric, tack and stitch. Turn up the hem and tack, but do not sew at this stage as curtains often drop a little after being hung and you will need to readjust the length. Next turn in the lining along side edges about 2 inches, press and slip-stitch to the curtain material. Hem the lower edge of the lining. Fix on heading tape according to type and instructions from manufacturer.

*Detachable curtain lining* Rufflette make a curtain lining tape for this type of lining, which is easy to apply. The tape is Y-shaped in section and the top of the lining fabric is sandwiched between the two sections of the tape which is then sewn in place. The drawstrings of the tape are pulled up just as in an ordinary curtain tape to give the correct width, and the curtain hooks are fixed first to the lining, then hooked on to the curtain ready for hanging.

*Curtain tapes and tracks* Now that attractive narrow and deep pleated headings can be easily produced using special tapes and hooks or simply tapes, there is no longer the need there used to be for pelmets or frills to hide the top of the curtain. Of course, you still may feel that in a very formal type of room a pelmet would be appropriate, or a frill in a pretty, feminine bedroom. Otherwise you can choose from a variety of heading tapes to give you simple gathered headings (some are specially made for nets or man-made fabrics); narrow pencil or pinch pleats; and deep pleated headings. There are now tapes available which will give you deep or narrow pinch pleats using just the ordinary curtain hooks. These are just as easy to stitch on as the simple 1-inch tape; and yet others in which you form the pleats—either single, double or triple—using a special type of pleater hook. Consult the style books and ask to see specimens of the tapes in use at your nearest large store.

When choosing your curtain track, bear in mind the window you are using it for and enquire if the track can be bent, if necessary, to follow the curve of an embrasure. On some types of track, if bent, the runners would tend to jam. You will find that there is a good choice of track, some in plastic which can be painted to match the room, some with a choice of stick-on trims, some in wood-veneered plastic and others in aluminium. Gliders can be metal or plastic—and if noise is a consideration, test a length in the shop for sound. Some tracks are double, thus enabling net curtains to be hung on the inner track; others overlap at the centre to allow the curtains to close completely; still others for a pelmet to be hung if necessary.

Make sure that the track you buy is strong enough for your curtain. A simple curtain wire would be perfectly suitable for hanging a net curtain, but would sag and be useless for a velvet one! The same applies to hooks—nylon and plastic ones are more suited to lighter fabrics.

A cording set (for use on straight tracks only) is a worthwhile investment. This means that you pull a cord at one side of the curtain only to draw them, thus lengthening the life of your curtain; no soiling or dragging from constant pulling and handling.

*You can achieve a stunning effect like this making your own curtains. This material is based on original Indian designs*

# Making Loose Covers

It is often possible to buy comfortable traditional arm-chairs and sofas very cheaply at auctions or in second-hand furniture shops, and these can be very much in keeping in large, older-type houses or do very well for the time being if they are not exactly what you want—given new covers. When you buy, make sure the springs are sound and there is no obvious evidence of moths, then choose your material and go ahead. It is not as difficult as it may seem to make a well-fitting loose cover.

*Measuring and materials*   As there is so much variation in the shape and size of traditional armchairs, it is only pos-sible to give approximate quantities of material needed. As a very rough guide, an average chair would require 6 yards of 48-inch fabric, plus an extra yard for a separate seat cushion and another yard allowance for matching if you choose a large pattern.

First take out the seat cushion, then measure up your chair as follows:

1. Back of the chair from top to floor.
2. Front of chair from top, down backrest, over seat and down to the floor.
3. Over each arm from the seat to the floor.

Add a further 5 inches for each tuck-in, inside arms and round the seat and an extra 4 inches on each piece for turnings. Make extra allowances as above if necessary. Piping will take another yard and you will also need about 12 yards of piping cord and hooks and eyes for fastening.

*Making the cover*   You can, of course, cut patterns from your chair out of brown paper to give you a guide for cutting out the fabric, and there is a good deal to be said for this if you are intending to keep the chair for a number of years and will be making new covers for it in the future.

Otherwise, the best plan is to cut out the fabric first in large pieces, roughly the right size, pinning them to the chair and obtaining the fit this way. It is easy to see where tuck-ins must be allowed for and you are not so liable to get the pieces mixed up. Pin the pieces right side out and to half the chair only, in order to match both sides.

First measure up to find the exact centre of the chair and mark it with a line of pins (A). Fold the pieces of material down the centre and place the folds to the pins (do not do this, however, to the arms and scrolls). When the pieces are pinned on, you can trim them so that they can be matched when taken off and re-pinned for stitching.

Cut the piece for the inside back. Lay the material on the chair, centring the pattern and allowing 5 inches tuck-in at the base and 2 inches beyond the top back. Then cut off complete width, fold in half down centre of pattern with right sides out, and lay in place on the chair (B). Next cut

outside back to within 4 inches of the floor, fold and pin along top to inside back (C).

Cut seat piece allowing 5 inches tuck-in at back and along sides and taking it over seat to within 2 inches of floor. As the seat edges will be piped, take a 2-inch pleat, cut it through the centre and pin pieces together again (D).

Cut the first inside arm piece, allowing a margin for the small part at the top which reaches round to the back of the chair and allowing tuck-in at seat edge and up inside arm. Cut the second arm piece from the first, matching the

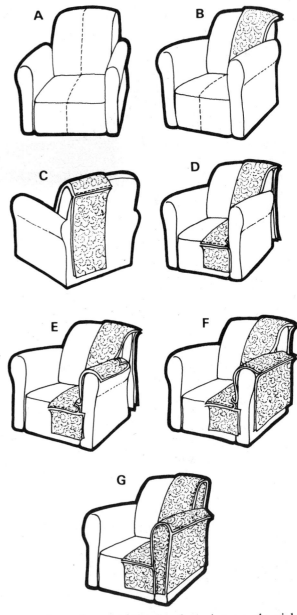

pattern beneath and laying the first piece on the right side of the material. Pin these pieces, wrong sides together, to the arm (E). Cut and pin on two outside arm pieces, so that they come to within 4 inches of the floor (F).

At the top inside of the arm, put a pin through inside arm and inside back piece and make a cut slantwise towards the pin through all raw edges so that you can fit the material round the chair back. Now cut two pieces each for side scrolls and front scrolls but do not shape them exactly. Cut with plenty of turning allowance and pin in pairs wrong sides facing (G).

Pin the tuck-ins round the seat and push in. Fit and adjust elsewhere, tapering where necessary. Clip any curves which are pulling. Trim all the turnings to $\frac{3}{4}$ inch then clip through all the thicknesses at intervals so that when you unpin you can match them up exactly. Mark 6 inches from the floor all round—the frill will be sewn along here.

Take off the cover pieces, unfold and pin together right sides facing, matching the notches.

Measure the seat cushion and cut top and bottom pieces, matching patterns to back piece. Cut border pieces for each side. Seam allowances should be $\frac{3}{4}$ inch all round. Cut and join together strips $7\frac{1}{2}$ inches deep until you have a piece to go $1\frac{1}{2}$ times round the edge of the cover, and press open seams. Make 12 yards of $1\frac{1}{2}$-inch strip, cut on the cross, for the piping.

Now machine together the tuck-ins round seat and up inside back. The other seams will be piped. Pipe the outer edges of the material all round, then stitch the corresponding edges to these. Unpin front scrolls first, pipe all round (except for bases) and pin back. Do the same for the side scrolls, but leave hanging from the back a length of piping long enough to reach the floor. Pin into the cover.

Pipe and stitch seat edge pieces and inside and outside arms together. Machine front scrolls in place. Pipe and stitch top of back. Machine in piped side scrolls, but leave one side of back open from within a few inches of the top to allow for fastening. Machine piping here to the single outside edge.

Cut a strip of fabric $2\frac{1}{2}$ inches wide on the straight for a facing, making it 3 inches longer than the opening. Turn in top and stitch one edge to the wrong side of the cover, turn in raw edge and machine down it. Neaten top and bottom turnings. Cut a strip 4 inches wide for strapping. Turn in top, then stitch one side to raw edge of opening, right sides facing. Make a small turning, fold strapping back to previous row of stitching and machine down it, neatening ends. Sew on hooks and eyes to fasten.

Pipe all round cover base along marked line. Hem base of frill strip and gather top, pulling it up to fit round cover base, including the facing. Turn in ends and finish. Machine on the frill.

For the cushion, stitch the four edge pieces into a cylinder and pipe both edges. Stitch to one cushion piece. Stitch on other piece, leaving all one side and half the adjoining side open. Cover raw edges on wrong sides of opening with facing strips and sew on hooks and eyes to close.

Press cover and fit it on your chair.

# Making Lampshades

Covering the type of lampshade frame you can buy in most big stores is largely a matter of patience and neat fingers. First the frame has to be bound using special lampshade tape (not bias binding), then a lining fitted and attached, and finally the cover made and fitted on. Some sort of trimming such as braid or fringing is often used to finish off the shade on the right side and cover stitching.

Detailed instructions for doing this will be found in many handicraft books and it is well worth investing in one if you are thinking of making most of the lampshades for your home. We are giving you instructions here for trying your hand at just two—the very popular lace Tiffany shade, which looks delightful in a bedroom, and a shade made in Raffene which would go anywhere in the house and can be copied in many attractive colours.

*Tiffany shade in lace*   You will need a Tiffany lampshade frame as a basis, and for one approximately 9 inches high, 4 inches across the top and $9\frac{1}{2}$ inches across the base you will need about $\frac{1}{2}$ yard cotton lace in the piece, 1 yard fringing, lampshade tape and a small tin of white enamel.

First paint the frame with white enamel and when it is dry bind the top and bottom rings with lampshade tape, by winding it tightly round and round, each turn of tape lying partly over the turn before. Measure the circumference of the frame and its depth, from top ring, down outside of strut to base ring.

Now cut a rectangular piece of lace 1 inch longer than the circumference and $1\frac{1}{4}$ inches deeper than the frame depth. Join the side edges together with a French seam (make a narrow seam with wrong sides of fabric facing, trim close, turn so that right sides are facing and take another narrow seam) so that a tube is formed which will fit tightly round the widest part of the frame.

Make a $\frac{1}{2}$-inch hem round the top of the lace tube, leaving a small opening. Run a fine string through the hem, leaving the ends sticking out, and place the cover over the frame with the seam lying down a strut. Draw up the string so that it fits the top ring. Lightly stretch down and pin the lace to the lower ring to hold it in place, then sew the lace hem to the binding on the top ring.

Unpin the lace from the lower ring, pull the cover tightly down over the frame and turn up the lower edge of the lace wrong side out, re-pinning it to the binding on the lower ring. Sew the lace firmly to the lower ring, then trim off the surplus lace. Sew on the fringe to cover the lower turned up edge, and stitch the fringe ends firmly together where they meet with tiny stitches. If you make your lace Tiffany in white and use a pink bulb in the shade, you will achieve a delightful rosy glow in your bedroom colour scheme.

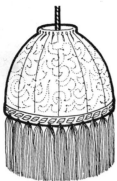

*Raffene-covered shade* You can cover any shaped shade in Raffene (the raffia-type craft material), but a globe shape looks particularly nice for living rooms and halls. First buy your shade, and when buying the Raffene ask the assistant

the correct amount for the size of shade (an 8-inch shade will take 2 skeins of Raffene). You will also need a tube of fabric adhesive.

First bind the top and bottom rings. Starting at a side stave, take a strand of Raffene round it, then bind tightly round the end and continue all round the ring. When you come back to the starting point, stick down the end of Raffene with a dab of adhesive. When you have bound both rings, fill in the shade as shown in Figures A, B and C.

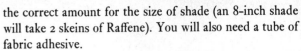
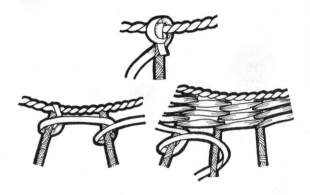

Tie the first strand of Raffene over the top ring at an upright (Fig. A), then take it behind the upright and out to the front. Take the strand along to the next upright, behind it and out to the front (Fig. B) and continue round and round the shade, keeping the rows just touching each other (Fig. C).

When you come to end of a strand stick the end unobtrusively inside it and start a new one by tying it to the same upright.

# HOUSEHOLD ACCESSORIES CHECKLIST

Here is a list of equipment, linen and household accessories which will be a useful check if you are moving into your own house or flat for the first time or, if you are about to get married, which you can send to friends with suggestions for wedding presents. It does not include such major items as chairs, beds, dining furniture and so on, but these will obviously have to figure in your preliminary budget.

First look through the list and mark with an asterisk those things which seem essential to you—obviously it will depend largely on your accommodation and budget. The rest can follow as funds allow. Then take the list round a local store and choose the make of china, glasses, cutlery etc. you and your husband or fiancé like, and fill this in under the column headed 'Make', adding under 'Details' the colour, pattern or any other identification needed. Under 'Number', fill in the quantity of each item you will need—for instance, how many cutlery place settings, glasses, etc.

Alternatively, you will find that many large stores have their own brides' service and check list which they will keep for you. You refer friends to the store and they then make a suggestion from your list and supply the present.

| Kitchen accessories | Make | Number | Details |
|---|---|---|---|
| Brooms and brushes (various) | | | |
| 1. | | | |
| 2. | | | |
| 3. | | | |
| 4. | | | |
| 5. | | | |
| Carpet sweeper | | | |
| Dustpan and brush | | | |
| Floor mop | | | |
| Waste bin | | | |
| Dustbin | | | |
| Kitchen step stool | | | |
| Ironing board | | | |
| Doormat | | | |
| Vegetable rack | | | |
| Timer | | | |
| Pepper mill | | | |
| Salt mill | | | |
| Grater | | | |
| Clothes horse | | | |
| Washing-up bowl | | | |

| Kitchen accessories | Make | Number | Details |
|---|---|---|---|
| Kitchen knives (various) | | | |
| 1. | | | |
| 2. | | | |
| 3. | | | |
| 4. | | | |
| 5. | | | |
| 6. | | | |
| Kitchen tools (various) | | | |
| 1. | | | |
| 2. | | | |
| 3. | | | |
| 4. | | | |
| 5. | | | |
| 6. | | | |
| Trays | | | |
| Wall can opener | | | |
| Kitchen scales | | | |
| Knife sharpener | | | |
| Kitchen scissors | | | |
| Pressure cooker | | | |
| Set of saucepans | | | |
| Frying pan | | | |
| Omelet pan | | | |
| Chip pan | | | |
| Double boiler | | | |
| Egg poacher | | | |
| Milk saucepan | | | |
| Casseroles | | | |
| Storage jars | | | |
| Spice rack | | | |
| Plate rack | | | |
| Bread bin | | | |
| Cake tins | | | |
| Flan tins | | | |
| Baking tray | | | |
| Tartlet tins | | | |
| Jelly moulds | | | |
| Mixing bowls | | | |
| Pie dishes | | | |
| Pastry board and rolling pin | | | |
| Salad bowl and servers | | | |
| Apple corer | | | |
| Bottle opener | | | |
| Bread board and knife | | | |
| Cheese board and knife | | | |
| Chopping board | | | |
| Carving dish | | | |

| Kitchen accessories | Make | Number | Details |
|---|---|---|---|
| Colander | | | |
| Sieve | | | |
| Strainer | | | |
| Mincer | | | |
| Juice extractor | | | |
| Measuring jug | | | |
| Corkscrew | | | |
| Flour bin | | | |
| Flour sifter | | | |
| Garlic press | | | |

| Linen | Make | Number | Details | Size |
|---|---|---|---|---|
| Sheets | | | | |
| Pillow cases | | | | |
| Blankets | | | | |
| Bedcovers | | | | |
| Eiderdowns | | | | |
| Continental quilts | | | | |
| Pillows | | | | |
| Tablecloths | | | | |
| Napkins | | | | |
| Mats | | | | |
| Traycloths | | | | |
| Bath towels | | | | |
| Face towels | | | | |
| Hand towels | | | | |
| Face cloths | | | | |
| Bath mats | | | | |
| Bathroom sets | | | | |
| Kitchen towels | | | | |
| Glass towels | | | | |
| Tea cloths | | | | |
| Floor cloths | | | | |
| Dish cloths | | | | |
| Dusters | | | | |

| Miscellaneous silver or stainless steel | Make | Number | Details |
|---|---|---|---|
| Cigarette box | | | |
| Condiment set | | | |
| Sauce boat | | | |
| Tea pot, sugar basin and cream jug | | | |
| Dishes (various) | | | |
|   1. | | | |
|   2. | | | |
|   3. | | | |
|   4. | | | |

| Miscellaneous silver or stainless steel | Make | Number | Details |
|---|---|---|---|
| Tea strainer | | | |
| Toast rack | | | |
| Coffee pot | | | |
| Sugar bowl | | | |
| Sugar sifter | | | |
| Sugar tongs | | | |

| Mechanical household equipment | Make | Design |
|---|---|---|
| Cooker | | |
| Hood | | |
| Extractor fan | | |
| Electric kettle | | |
| Food mixer | | |
| Refrigerator | | |
| Home freezer | | |
| Washing machine | | |
| Spin dryer | | |
| Dishwasher | | |
| Vacuum cleaner | | |
| Floor polisher | | |
| Toaster | | |
| Coffee percolator | | |
| Coffee grinder | | |
| Tea maker | | |
| Hotplate or trolley | | |
| Iron | | |
| Electric blanket | | |
| Room heaters (various) | | |
|   1. | | |
|   2. | | |
|   3. | | |
|   4. | | |
| Lamps (various) | | |
|   1. | | |
|   2. | | |
|   3. | | |
|   4. | | |

| China | Make | Number | Details |
|---|---|---|---|
| Breakfast service | | | |
| Tea set | | | |
| Dinner service | | | |
| Coffee set | | | |
| Fruit set | | | |
| Tea pot | | | |

| China | Make | Number | Details |
|---|---|---|---|
| Milk jug and sugar basin | | | |
| Butter dish | | | |
| Egg cups | | | |
| Mugs or beakers | | | |
| Marmalade jar | | | |
| Jam dish | | | |

**Glass**

Sherry glasses
Tumblers (water)
Wine glasses
  (for red and white wine)
Special glasses for:
  Brandy
  Champagne
  Liqueurs
  Whisky
Decanter
Water jug
Vase
Fruit bowl (large)
Fruit bowls (small)
Every-day glasses

**Cutlery**

Place settings
Fish eaters
Serving spoons
  and forks
Ladle (large)
Ladle (small)
Teaspoons
Coffee spoons
Steak knives
Carving knife
  and fork
Butter knife
Cheese knife
Jam spoon

| Mechanical household equipment | Make | Design |
|---|---|---|
| Radio | | |
| Record player | | |
| Tape recorder | | |
| Television set | | |
| Electric towel rail | | |
| Hair dryer | | |

| Miscellaneous home needs | Make | Number | Details |
|---|---|---|---|
| Ashtrays | | | |
| Bath rack | | | |
| Bathroom scales | | | |
| Bathroom cabinet | | | |
| Bathroom accessories | | | |
| Clock | | | |
| Cushions | | | |
| Garden chairs | | | |
| Garden tools (various) | | | |
|   1. | | | |
|   2. | | | |
|   3. | | | |
|   4. | | | |
| Linen basket | | | |
| Mirror | | | |
| Picnic basket | | | |
| Pouffe | | | |
| Record rack | | | |
| Rugs (various) | | | |
|   1. | | | |
|   2. | | | |
|   3. | | | |
|   4. | | | |
| Sewing machine | | | |
| Shopping basket | | | |
| Typewriter | | | |
| Stepladder | | | |
| Table mats | | | |
| Tool kit | | | |
| Trolley | | | |
| Vacuum flasks | | | |
| Vases | | | |
| Waste-paper baskets | | | |
| Wine racks | | | |

# BUDGET LIST

If the full list seems rather formidable to you, here is a basic list of necessities on which it would be perfectly possible to manage at first. You do need a cooker, but you don't need a refrigerator; you don't need every saucepan size there is, but what you have should be good and from a range which can be added to later; your kitchen knives may be few, but make sure they are the best you can afford and they will, with later additions, last you many years. The same goes for items such as bed linen.

## Linen

2 pairs double sheets or
    4 pairs single sheets
8 pillow cases
4 pillows
2 double blankets
    or 4 single blankets
or: 1 double continental quilt
    and 2 covers
1 bedcover or 2 single ones
2 large towels
4 medium towels
2 tablecloths or sets of mats
1 bath mat
4 tea towels

## China and glass

6 plates each of dinner,
    pudding and tea sizes
6 medium tea or coffee cups
    and saucers
2 large mugs
2 egg cups
6 bowls
Salt and pepper
6 tumblers
6 wine glasses
Glass jug
Tea pot
Coffee pot
Milk jug
Sugar bowl

## Cutlery

6 place settings
4 serving spoons
Carving knife and fork
6 tea/coffee spoons

## Kitchen needs

1 large and 1 medium saucepan
1 milk saucepan
1 large frying pan
2 casseroles
2 mixing bowls
8 storage jars, various sizes
Pastry board and rolling pin
1 pie dish
1 baking tray
1 flan ring
2 sandwich tins
Mixing spoon
Kitchen scales
Kitchen tool set
Whisk
Kitchen knives; vegetable knife,
    utility knife, bread knife
Coffee percolator
Colander
Grater
Tin opener
Corkscrew
Pepper mill
Mincer
Plate rack
Rubbish bin
Kitchen stool/steps
Ironing board
Linen basket
Wooden clothes horse
Dusters
Mop
Dust pan and brush
Broom
Dustbin
Polythene bowls (2)

## Large items

Cooker
Carpet sweeper or
    vacuum cleaner
Iron
Room heaters
Lamps

# YOUR PERSONAL TELEPHONE LIST

If something goes wrong in your household—someone has an accident, a water tank bursts, or the television set breaks down just before the Cup Final, you will want to save precious minutes by having these telephone numbers ready. Enter them in pencil

Dentist .............

Doctor .............

Hairdresser .............

Optician .............

Veterinary surgeon .............

Welfare clinic .............

Agent handling repairs for

    Cooker .............

    Dishwasher .............

    Home freezer .............

    Refrigerator .............

    Vacuum cleaner .............

    Washing machine .............

Builder .............

Car service garage .............

Coal merchant .............

Dressmaker .............

Electrician .............

Electricity Board .............

Equipment hire shop .............

Furniture remover or carrier .............

Gas Board .............

Insurance agent or broker .............

Oil company (heating fuels) .............

Parcels office, British Rail .............

Plumber .............

Railway Station .............

School(s) .............

Sports and social clubs .............

Town Hall (or RDC offices) .............

TV rental/repair firm .............

Water Board .............

# RESERVE STORES

No sudden influx of visitors, forgotten early closing day or family crisis can catch you unawares if you keep a stock of basic foodstuffs and more exciting things that can make a meal in a moment. You will probably want to make your own selection from the following items, building up your store cupboard as you go along.

**Dry stores**

Baking powder

Beans: dried, butter, haricot

Bicarbonate of soda

Biscuits: sweet, semi-sweet, chocolate, cheese, crispbread, water biscuits

Breakfast cereals: at least two varieties

Cheese, Parmesan

Cornflour

Cream of tartar

Custard powder

Dried fruits: apricots, candied peel, currants, dates, figs, glacé cherries, prunes, raisins, sultanas

Dried yeast

Essences: almond, anchovy, lemon, vanilla

Flour: plain, self-raising and wholemeal

Gelatine

Herbs: bay leaves, celery seed, marjoram, mixed herbs, mint, oregano, parsley, sage, thyme

Instant pudding mixes

Jelly cubes

Lentils

Meat-extract cubes

Nuts, shelled: almonds, hazelnuts, peanuts, pistachio

Oatmeal: medium and rolled oats

Pasta: lasagne, macaroni, shells and other shapes, spaghetti, vermicelli

Pastry mix

Peas, dried

Pepper: black and white peppercorns, cayenne, paprika

Rice: long-grain, Patna, unpolished

Salt: sea, rock crystals, table

Semolina

Spices and flavourings: allspice, caraway seeds, chilli powder, cinnamon, cloves, coriander, cummin seeds, ginger, ground and root; mace, whole and ground; mixed spice, nutmeg, turmeric, vanilla pods

Stuffings: packets of parsley & thyme and sage & onion

Sugar: Barbados, caster, Demerara, granulated, icing, loaf, lump, preserving, soft brown

Tapioca

**Beverages**
Bedtime malted and milk drinks
Cocoa
Chocolate powder
Coffee: bags, beans, bottled and instant
Meat extract, bottled
Milk powder
Tea, tea bags

**Preserves, etc.**
Chutneys
Golden syrup
Honey, clear and crystallised
Jam, a selection
Jelly: bramble, crabapple, redcurrant
Lemon curd
Marmalade
Mayonnaise
Mincemeat
Olive oil and other cooking oils
Salad cream
Sauces: barbecue, horseradish, mint, table sauce, tartare, tomato, Worcester
Vinegars: cider, distilled, malt, tarragon, wine, white and red

**Tinned goods**
Cream
Fish: anchovies, crab, kipper fillets, pilchards, salmon, sardines, soft roes, tuna
Fruit: a selection of berries, currants, stone fruits and citrus fruits

Fruit juices
Meat: corned beef, ham, meat loaf, pâté, stewed steak, tongue
Milk: condensed, evaporated
Soup: a selection of consommé, meat, fish and vegetable soups
Vegetables: asparagus tips, beans, baked and green; beetroot, carrots, celery hearts, mixed vegetables, pimientoes, new potatoes, potato salad, sweet corn, kernels and creamed; tomatoes; tomato purée, vegetable salad
Puddings: creamed rice pudding, instant milk puddings, steamed puddings

**Perishable goods**
Bacon
Butter
Cheese: cottage, cream and a selection of British and foreign cheeses
Cooked meats
Cream, double and single
Eggs
Fish
Margarine
Meat
Milk
Yoghurt, plain and fruit-flavoured

NOTE: In households where there is a home freezer, many of the items suggested, such as fruit, vegetables and pastry dishes, would be frozen instead of dried or tinned.

# EMERGENCY SPARES

It is always on Sunday or during a public holiday period that something vital is needed that isn't in the house and can't be bought, such as a large sticking plaster or a spare electric light bulb. This page will, we hope, act as a reminder for some, at least, of those small things which become necessary from time to time in the running of a home.

**First Aid**  Buy a kit ready packed (any chemist can supply one), or fill a box yourself. You will need:
Assorted plasters
Roll of plaster to cut (there are never enough large sizes in the average tin)
Bandage
Bottle of antiseptic
Anti-histamine cream (for insect bites)
Cottonwool
Aspirin (or similar)
Alka Seltzer (or the equivalent)
Travel sickness pills
Small bottle of brandy (strictly medicinal!)
Your pet cough or cold cure

**Electrical Repairs**  These should, of course, be limited to minor jobs such as changing a plug and repairing a fuse. Anything major needs professional attention. Keep in a handy place (top of the fuse box) the following:
Torch (the lights have all fused!)
Electrical screwdriver
Card of fuse wire
One or two spare plugs
Packet of fuses
Sharp, protected blade
Roll of insulating tape

**Handyman Jobs**  Your husband will probably deal with odd jobs such as picture hanging, and so on, but in case he is not the handyman type with his own well-organised tool kit, you may find it useful to have some of the following in a convenient drawer:
Hammer with claw end (for pulling out nails as well as hammering)
Assortment of nails and screws
Picture hooks and wire
Screwdriver (the kind with one handle and an assortment of ends to screw in is useful)
Bradawl
Pair of pliers
Sharp knife
Old knife
Clamps
Rawlplug, Polyfilla or similar
Assortment of glues
Metal measuring tape

**Stain Removal**  See guide on pages 79–82.

**Miscellaneous**  Set aside a cupboard shelf for all those odds and ends which are small in themselves, but vital when you do need them.
Spare electric light and torch bulbs
Spare torch batteries
Candles and matches (those power cuts again!)
Lighter fuel
String
Pair of scissors (you've mislaid all the other ones in the house)
Drawing pins
Wrapping paper and string
Spare birthday card and paper (there will come a day when one of you forgets a birthday)
Book of stamps

# THINKING METRIC

Metrication, whether we like the idea or not, is with us to stay, and the conversion tables given on this page will be useful for reference when you have to make close conversions. However, if you can cultivate the habit of working out approximate equivalents from Imperial to Metric it will be a great help round the house and in the shops. Length, volume and weight are the three measurements with which the housewife will be mainly concerned; as far as temperature is concerned, Centigrade has been with us for some long time, and one is beginning to feel that 25 degrees C is a nice warm summer day!

## Length

Approximations to remember:

  1 yard = just under 1 metre
  1 foot = just over 30 centimetres
  1 inch = about $2\frac{1}{2}$ centimetres
  10 yards = about 9 metres
  100 yards = about 90 metres

Linear conversion table:

  1 inch = 2·54 centimetres
  1 foot = 30·48 centimetres
  1 yard = 0·9144 metre
  1 mile = 1·6093 kilometres

Rulers and tape measures are available which give both types of measurement.

## Volume

Capacity, which is now measured in fluid ounces, pints and gallons will be measured in millilitres and litres (1,000 millilitres = 1 litre). You are probably quite familiar with the 5 millilitres measuring spoon for medicine, which has been in use in this country for some time.

Approximations to remember:

  1 fluid ounce = about 28·5 millilitres
  1 pint = about 0·56 litre (or 568 millilitres)—in other words 1 litre = about $1\frac{3}{4}$ pints
  1 gallon = about $4\frac{1}{2}$ litres

Capacity conversion table:

  1 pint = 0·568 litre
  1 quart = 1·136 litres
  1 gallon = 4·546 litres

## Weight

The basic unit of weight will be the kilogramme, which comprises 1,000 grammes, each gramme being the equivalent of $\frac{1}{30}$ of an ounce.

Approximations to remember:

  1 pound = approximately $\frac{1}{2}$ kilogramme
  1 hundredweight = approximately 50 kilogrammes

More exactly:

  1 ounce = 28·350 grammes
  1 pound = 0·453592 kilogramme
  1 stone = 6·350 kilogrammes
  1 cwt = 50·80 kilogrammes
  1 ton = 1·0160 tonnes or 1016 kilogrammes

# USEFUL ADDRESSES

The Home Economist, Prestige Group Limited, 14–18 Holborn, London, E.C.1.

The National Heating Centre, 34 Mortimer Street, London W.1.

Insulation Glazing Association, 6 Mount Row, London W.1.

Rentokil Advice Centre, 16 Dover Street, London W.1. Home Insulation Service, also advice on woodworm, damp-proofing, etc.

ICI Insulation Service Ltd., Rosanne House, Bridge Road, Welwyn Garden City, Herts.

The Building Centre, 26 Store Street, London W.C.2.

Air Improvement Services, 21 Napier Road, Bromley, Kent. (Humidifier information.)

National Bedding Federation, 251 Brompton Road, London S.W.3. (Leaflets on beds and bedding.)

British Carpet Centre, Dorland House, 14–16 Lower Regent Street, London S.W.1.

Scotchgard, 3M House, Wigmore Street, London W.1. (Advice on stain-resistant treatment for furniture.)

The Design Centre, 28 Haymarket, London W.1.

Electrical information: consult your local district office or showrooms.

British Gas, 59 Bryanston Street, London W.1.

Solid fuel: advice is available through regional offices of the Solid Fuel Advisory Service. For name of local branch, contact the Domestic Branch, Marketing Dept., National Coal Board, Hobart House, Grosvenor Place, London S.W.1.

Shell-Mex and BP Ltd., Trade Relations Dept., Shell-Mex House, The Strand, London W.C.2. (Central heating.)

Esso Petroleum Co. Ltd., Esso House, Victoria Street, London SWIE 5JW. (Central heating.)

The Glass Manufacturers Federation, 19 Portland Place, London W.1. (Enquiries on domestic glassware.)

The National Association of Furniture Warehousemen and Removers, Ltd., 39 Victoria Street, London S.W.1.

The British Assurance Association, Aldermary House, Queen Street, London E.C.4.

For leaflets, booklets, general advice and information on the products of member companies, write to:

The Domestic Refrigeration Development Committee (refrigerators)

The Dishwasher Development Council (dishwashers)

The Food Freezer Committee (home freezers)
all at 25 North Row, London W.1.

# BOOKS TO HELP YOU

*Teach Yourself Home Heating* by B. J. King and J. E. Beer. This is not a textbook on do-it-yourself central heating, but a comprehensive general guide to the subject. (Teach Yourself series, 55p.)

*Woman's Weekly Around the House* How to make soft furnishings and lampshades. (IPC Magazines publication, 15p.)

Design Centre publications, all at 60p. from the Design Centre, 28 Haymarket, London SW1Y 4SU (postage and packing extra):

*Lighting* by Derek Phillips

*Tableware* by Elizabeth Good

*Flooring* by Derek Phillips

*Kitchens* by John Prizeman

*Living Rooms* by Mary and Neville Ward

*Storage* by Geoffrey Salmon

*Bathrooms* by Gontran Goulden

*Bedrooms* by Dorothy Meade

*Saving and Home Buying*—a guide by Norman Griggs. (Published for the Building Societies Association, 15p.)

*Home Guide to Deep Freezing* by Audrey Ellis. (Published by Hamlyn, £1·05.)

*The Freezer Book* by Marye Cameron-Smith. (Published by Elm Tree Books, £2·10.)

*Pressure Cooking Day by Day* by Mrs. K. F. Broughton. (Published by Kaye and Ward, £2·00.)

# INDEX